The Structure of
Byron's Major Poems

THE STRUCTURE OF
BYRON'S MAJOR POEMS

by

William H. Marshall

University of Pennsylvania Press
Philadelphia

Library of Congress Catalog Card Number: 62-17305
ISBN (paper): 0-8122-1078-6

Printed in the United States of America

For my daughters
Judith, Sue, and Barbara

Contents

Preface

THIS BOOK EMBODIES THE RESULTS OF SOME YEARS OF ABIDING interest in the poetry of Lord Byron. That Byron as a person and a figure in English literary history has absorbed the attention of writers from his time to ours is obviously supported by the enormous number of books and articles which have been written about him, including of course my own earlier work on his connection with *The Liberal*. Some writers have ventured into the question of the nature and quality of his poetry, but few have tried to answer it directly. In the course of time I have become strongly persuaded that this question must be concerned first with the structure of the poems, and upon this very firm assumption I have written my book. It is intended to be neither more nor less than its title proposes, a work which I hope may usefully serve students of literature in their attempt to move toward a detached judgment of Byron's poetry.

My indebtedness is large. First, I wish to acknowledge the Research Grant awarded me for the summer of 1960 by the Committee on the Advancement of Research of the University of Pennsylvania, which made it possible for me to re-examine and organize my thoughts about these poems in preparation for the writing of the book. For both professional and personal encouragement I am most grateful to Professor Otto Springer, Dean of the College of the University of Pennsylvania, to Professor Matthias A. Shaaber, former Chairman of the Department of English, and to Professors Frederick L. Jones and Allan G. Chester, each of whom has served as Graduate Chairman of English during the preparation and writing of this book. I wish to thank many of my colleagues at Pennsylvania for their friendly support and occasional suggestions, particularly Professors Albert C. Baugh, Maurice Johnson, Morse Peckham, Clyde de L. Ryals, Arthur H. Scouten, and Harold S. Stine. I am indebted to the members of English 650, my graduate lecture course on Byron, who, during the fall term of 1960, listened patiently to my development of some of the ideas which take their final form in this book. The editors of *Modern Language Notes* and of *The Personalist* have kindly given permission to reprint portions of articles appearing in their journals during 1961, respectively "A Reading of Byron's *Mazeppa*" and "Byron's *Parisina* and the Function of Psychoanalytic Criticism."

My most personal debt for understanding and encouragement is to my father and mother, Robert and Nettie Marshall, to the three girls to whom the book is dedicated, and of course to my wife, Shirl.

W. H. M.

Cynwyd, Pennsylvania
August 1962

The Structure of
Byron's Major Poems

I

Introduction

BYRON HAS BEEN IGNORED MORE THAN ANY OTHER MAJOR RO-
mantic poet by the modern critics. The literary biographers,
the historians, and the editors have, in varying degrees, dealt
successfully with him as a personality, as a figure in literary
history, or with the texts of his poems. In their attempts to
make critical judgments of his poetry they have followed
certain patterns which in turn have frequently prevented
them from studying the poems with significant objectivity.
The dominant view of Byron's work has been exclusively
biographical. This was initially encouraged of course by
Byron himself, who made the article in the *Edinburgh Review*
a personal matter, allowed the public to confuse Harold and
his creator, and throughout his career pointedly used his art
for cathartic purposes. "Manfred is merely himself, with a
fancy-drapery on," Hazlitt wrote shortly before Byron's death.[1]
And since that time most, though not all, of those who have
attempted to make critical comments upon Byron's poetry
have become too frequently involved in the quest for biographical references in the poetry itself. The result has been
a kind of judgment that is essentially neither biographical
nor critical. Most of those who pursue a dominantly, or exclusively, biographical approach to the poetry of Byron offer
no apology; in fact, of these all would reject the idea that any
other is necessary. Yet even those who set out to study the
poems with the full intention of restricting the biographical
element to reasonable critical bounds frequently find them-

selves very much in the position of Mr. Dick regarding King Charles's head.[2]

Another established pattern in Byron studies, also arising principally from a consideration of the poetry as necessarily deriving from the poet as a conscious personality, is expressed in the quest for meaning, especially of theological or ethical value, in the poems. This most frequently blocks a view of *Manfred* or *Cain* as works of art, particularly when one imposes viewpoints upon either poem which are essentially extrinsic to it.[3] A third area for the Byronist has been the study of sources, prominently for the Tales and *Don Juan,* and of Byron's influence upon the work of others. Closely related is the interest of social and philosophic historians, best demonstrated by Bertrand Russell perhaps,[4] in the significance of "Byronism" in the socio-cultural history of the last century and a half.

All of these views of Byron's work either prepare for or assume a reading of the poetry itself, but none of them really offers just that. T. S. Eliot, one of the few modern critics who has dealt expressly with Byron (though most generally of course), proposes a reason for the neglect: "he has been admired for what are his most ambitious attempts to be poetic; and these attempts turn out, on examination, to be fake: nothing but sonorous affirmations of the commonplace with no depth of significance." [5] Eliot, whose position places him within the moralist tradition of Byron critics, poses (and probably begs) the question of the nature of Byron's positive assertions and the necessarily related question of the possibility of Byron's acceptance of a "System." The poet himself, writing to R. C. Dallas, once asserted that he had read more philosophy than he could understand.[6] But this should not be taken too literally or pursued too conclusively, for it is another instance of Byron's ironic modesty concerning his own capacities, one of those clues that have been so badly magnified by critics who seem bent upon demonstrating that the poet was a kind of fortunate idiot.

Actually, Byron was a figure set apart from any direct participation in a tradition of belief or developing intellectual position. His religious training was Anglican, with a strong infusion of Calvinism. He did not have an emotional awareness of the cosmos of medieval Christianity, and he seems to have regarded Renaissance Humanism as a force now belonging primarily to cultural history. He was to some extent familiar with, but presumably unaffected by, the teachings of the Age of Reason. Nor was he to become an affirmer of any of those systems or viewpoints which are peculiarly nineteenth-century contributions to human thought —the essentially bourgeois principles of a Bentham or a Mill, the intellectualist ideal of a Shelley, the dialectical system of a Marx. He recognized the inadequacies of the social and intellectual systems which he knew, but in his letters and journals he offered comments upon, rather than substitutes for, these systems. Throughout his life he failed to give affirmation to any structure of faith or any complex of belief. He was unable to find and accept an intellectual basis for existence as an absolutist, and at the same time he appears to have been emotionally incapable of subscribing to relativism as a position for an essentially positive view of existence.[7] His being seems to reflect a fundamental split between skepticism and the impulse to believe and belong.

Thus, though a classicist by assertion, Byron was not primarily one in practice, for the essential quality of the kind of art that we identify with the Augustan Age in England demands acceptance of an order, albeit an ideal rather than a real order, the meaning of which can be ironically affirmed by one's attack upon disorder. That Byron did not, apparently could not, give his acceptance to the proposition that such an order prevails is sometimes offered as the reason for his limited success in such works modeled upon classic forms as *Hints from Horace* and *The Age of Bronze*. Presumably as he recognized this fact about his own emotional capacities, he began to emerge as the poet of *Beppo* and *Don Juan*. He abandoned his quest for meaning in Nature and the Universe[8] and accepted failure (perhaps thereby paradoxically achieving a degree of success) in his pursuit of an integration of the self. On occasion Byron is described in this final phase of his work as once more "classical." But such is hardly the case. By 1817, when he wrote *Beppo*, he had largely accepted imperfection in the Self and in Man's consciousness as an end in itself rather than as an obstacle in one's view of life that somehow had to be got around. He had become, in other words, an ironist,[9] one aware of the limits of human capacity and the absurdity of many forms of human activity, but in exposing these he was offering no suggestion for an ideal substitute in human behavior, as the satirist implicitly does. He became, instead, the delight of the fundamental human type which Gilbert Murray called "the anarchist," one who

laughs to see the Clown burning the Policeman with the hot poker, or the cinema hero knocking people into tubs of whitewash, just as in ancient Athens he joined in flinging mockery at magistrates and generals and divine beings; as in the Middle Ages he used to dance in the Feast of Fools and mock at bishops and nuns and the holy chalice itself. He identifies himself with the rascalities of some Xanthias or Sosias or Scapin, and the irresponsible mystifications of Figaro and Don Cézar de Bazan. He sides shamelessly with the young lovers who deceive and rob sundry meritorious persons, such as guardians and creditors, and in general all the elderly and orderly.[10]

Essentially, then, we must not seek sustaining, positive meaning in Byron's poetry. On the other hand, we should hesitate before we accept as ultimately significant the position of Mr. Eliot, that Byron's poetry contains only "sonorous" but superficial "affirmations of the commonplace." Mr. Eliot appears, in his criticism of Byron, to be building largely upon what Cleanth Brooks calls "the paraphrastic heresy," which Mr. Brooks defines as the belief that "we can conceive the purpose of a poem to be only the production, in the end, of a proposition—of a statement." [11] To the critical heretics in Mr. Brooks's consideration, nothing else in a poem, or in any other work of art for that matter, is of importance beyond its explicit meaning; or to put the case another way, the poem is as good as its meaning, and all the rest counts for nothing. The only possible criterion would then be the importance of the statement contained in the poem, and a writer like Byron who makes no such statements would be, indeed, no poet. There is, in other words, no reconciliation between this critical position and Byron's performance.

But the concern of Mr. Brooks and the Byronists should be somewhat limited, for there are now fewer paraphrastic heretics than there used to be. Modern critics, despite extremes and absurdities to which on occasion they have been led by either untested assumptions or unrestricted enthusiasms, have made it abundantly and persuasively clear to all but the most inflexible that there are indeed various elements to look for in a poem besides its central proposition in order to make a qualitative judgment concerning that poem.

We assume, then, that when a poem *can* be reduced to a statement without appreciable loss of force, it is not a poem of quality. And at this point it should be admitted that many of Byron's poems are, for this very reason, not to be regarded as poems of quality. Such is the case with a number of the lyrics, in which literal assertions are bound together by a common theme, though there are some exceptions ("So We'll Go No More A-Roving," "Stanzas Written on the

Road between Florence and Pisa," "On This Day I Complete My Thirty-sixth Year"). In the many occasional verses, those frequently contained in letters to John Murray or Thomas Moore, the momentary surprise often achieved at the conclusion does not sufficiently complement the easily paraphrased personal assertion or the dominant commonplace. Despite nearly a century and a half of supposed popular esteem and a degree of academic praise, the stricture applies largely to the first two cantos of *Childe Harold's Pilgrimage* and to the supposedly conventional satires, *English Bards and Scotch Reviewers* and *Hints from Horace*. There are of course other poems, or parts thereof, but a catalogue is not my intention. It is sufficient to remark that the excellent poetry in the Byron canon, outside of *Don Juan,* is clearly quite limited.

On the other hand, many of the poems frequently regarded as badly contrived and trivial, even worthless, have merits that are not generally recognized. Though in themselves, in certain instances, these qualities do not render the poems excellent, they become, when subsequently used and developed in other poems, qualities of excellence. The point is, quite simply, that though Byron does indeed become the ironist of *Don Juan,* he is not suddenly equipped to do so as he accepts imperfection in the Self and in its view of the Universe, as our proposition might at first suggest.

The proposal that Byron developed in his art requires that we deal, as others on occasion have already dealt, with one of the most persistent heresies about Byron—that his aesthetic creation was a kind of accident. It is a heresy to which Byron himself of course first gave much support—in his statements regarding the rapid composition of certain of the Tales, in his jokes about the indefinite course of "Donny Johnny," and in fact in his rather consistent pose as a kind of latter-day Cavalier Poet. Biographers, both his contemporaries and ours, have done the rest, reconstructing many times over the image of the lonely man inspired by Teresa Guiccioli, or gin and water, or almost anything of the moment, compulsively releasing his tensions by setting forth whatever possessed him. Like most legends, this has a nucleus, but no more, of truth. There is, particularly in his early work, evidence of indifference to the externals of form, in some instances revealed by mechanical accretion through several editions without any attempt at organic revision. And temperamentally, it is true, Byron was not basically disposed toward such attempts. To insist upon this indifference as a total causative factor, however, is to confuse the social being, the poseur (which perhaps all social beings are), with the solitary artist, the personality which at times seemed to exist on an animal level of being, with the creator who occasionally achieved heights.[12] Ultimately, then, the assertion must remain a heresy, as Truman Guy Steffan's detailed study, in *The Making of a Masterpiece,* of the revision of *Don Juan* should demonstrate to us.[13]

Another matter remains—the question of the relation between the poet's intentions and the achievement of poetry. As soon as a suggestion concerning Byron's development is introduced, the question is posed: did the poet "intend" to bring to certain of his poems considered as part of this development the elements, ironic or otherwise, that we seem to discover there? To say that he did intend to do this, or rather that his work in the poems never transcended the limits of his intentions, is to return to a point very near that at which begins the paraphrastic heresy: it is to propose that the fulfillment of his intentions can be equated to the achievement of the poem, therefore that a description of these intentions is similar, if not equal, to a description of the poem itself. Those who have made such "descriptions" regarding, say, *Paradise Lost, The Rime of the Ancient Mariner,* or *Prome-*

theus Unbound have of course concluded by treating these works as if they were simple allegories, each of whose symbols possesses one fixed meaning as precisely intended by the poet. It seems reasonable (and this will be the viewpoint underlying the studies that follow) to propose instead that intention yields the subject, the general form, and the meaning of the poem; but organic creation, an activity that takes place primarily in the subconscious, begins where conscious and mechanical intention ceases. No work of literature was ever written that was not first constructed upon the writer's fixed and regulating intention toward that work; but no significant literary work ever failed to rise above this base, to become for the writer himself "something rich and strange" in the very process of creation. In terms of this, the critic's function is primarily to give some conscious explanation of what goes on in the work itself (presumably, then, reflecting what has gone on in the mind of the writer) at a somewhat less than conscious level.[14]

It is of course not new to suggest that in some of Byron's poetry the dominant element is irony. It is, however, a fact that has generally been overlooked that in certain of his poems, especially some of those written from 1816 onward, the element is characteristically dramatic irony.[15] This offers sustaining structural unity to perhaps half a dozen major poems written between 1816 and 1819, and is given its most complex development in *Don Juan*. Dramatic irony, as the phrase is used here, is achieved in a work by the apparent discrepancy between the speaker's intended and actual revelations. In the simple, the usual, dramatic monologue, there is of course one speaker; in *Don Juan* there are many, an apparently indefinite number, merging one into another in a continual kaleidoscopic motion that is sustained throughout the poem.

It is probably justifiable to assert that every poem has a

speaker, but in many poems the speaker, indistinct from the poet in *any* way, becomes no more than an impersonal narrator and occasionally a dispassionate commentator upon scene or action. Only when this speaker assumes a distinct, identifiable personality, which exists fully within the bounds of the work itself, can the poem in any sense be called a dramatic monologue. Irony becomes a quality of the poem, in this instance dramatic irony, when the reader, interpreting what the speaker says in terms of either common reason or information revealed to the reader but presumably not understood by the speaker himself, becomes aware of the discrepancy between appearance and reality. In his discussion of paradox, Cleanth Brooks has remarked, "The dramatization demands that the antithetical aspects of memory be coalesced into one entity which—if we take it on the level of statement—is a paradox, the assertion of the union of opposites." [16] What has been called the "Byronic Hero," whose essence is expressed by his inability either to worship or to accept guilt, becomes an ideal subject for dramatic irony. The Byronic cosmos, constituted somehow of neither credible absolutism nor acceptable relativism, is essentially one of paradox needing expression by dramatization. Most readers have long recognized both the dramatic and the ironic elements in *Don Juan,* though they have generally failed to discover the relation (or even *that* there is a relation) between these elements. But few have regarded the poems preceding *Don Juan,* particularly the so-called Tales, the monologues,[17] and certainly *Manfred,* as anything but expressions of Byron's own emotional situation; they have failed to see that in these poems (and perhaps ultimately this is the real significance of many of them) he developed the dramatic and ironic techniques that were to be used with greatest aesthetic integrity in *Don Juan.*

Among Byron's early poems there are but few which approach the dramatic method. In the first two cantos of *Childe Harold's Pilgrimage* the speaker appears not to become distinct from the author; the poem, though ostensibly a narrative, is essentially descriptive, concerned primarily with the supposed affects of his experiences upon Harold, who seldom actually moves as a character and frequently seems to lack motivation. *The Curse of Minerva* approaches a dramatic form, since within its Chinese-box structure the speaker recalls the apparition of Minerva and the curse that she uttered against those Englishmen under Lord Elgin who were removing the Marbles from Greece; neither the narrator nor Minerva herself, however, is really identifiable except in terms of the literal meaning of what each proclaims. In *The Giaour,* that unduly long work of many fragments rather than one, Bryon first achieves dramatic irony: the simple Moslem fisherman who narrates the major incident of the early phase of the episode, the Giaour's killing of the Moslem Prince Hassan, reveals far more than he himself realizes of his intense hatred for the Christian stranger. But through seven editions Byron indulged in so much mechanical accretion without any organic revision that the dramatic tension established by the fisherman's speeches in the manuscript version of *The Giaour* is totally dissipated.[18] The Tales, simple in structure and yet rather abundant in incident, are primarily narrative rather than dramatic in method. In *Lara,* however, we are aware of a speaker, the narrator, who is not completely lost as a personality in the incidents which he recounts. *Parisina* represents a departure, for within the simple narrative of the deadly struggle between father and son, the two principals indulge in long speeches, any one of which achieves a substantial degree of dramatic irony. The year 1815, in which Byron wrote *Parisina,* closes what might be called the "First Phase" of his work; here we find much poetry that is not only essentially undramatic in structure but frequently even confessional, expressing an emotionally directed, almost childish, quest for a kind of earthly perfection which, presumably, the poet himself was seeking.

The following year, 1816, for reasons which I do not pretend to understand but would not necessarily attribute to the separation from Lady Byron,[19] opens what I arbitrarily call the "Middle Phase," the qualities of which are to be found in most of the poems written through 1818 and in some of those composed thereafter; only *Don Juan* constitutes what I should call the "Final Phase" (for which reason I have hesitated to use the word "Period" in making these divisions). In the poems written in and after 1816, the poet demonstrated his growing acceptance of imperfection in man's capacities and of disorder in human affairs as the basis for sublimational order in art: in his major poems of the Middle Phase Byron dramatized the ironic situations of those who were essentially unable to reconcile themselves to imperfection.

The protagonists in these poems are of two sorts—first, those who fail in their attempts to remake their visions of the world and therefore cease to struggle toward resolution; secondly, those who appear to succeed only because they alter the nature of the Self and the view of the world which the Self imposes. In the first group I should place the protagonist in *Manfred*. As several others have already pointed out, the work is essentially a sustained soliloquy, in which characters other than Manfred himself appear either as little more than projections of his own consciousness or, in the case of the Chamois Hunter and the Abbot of St. Maurice, as functional ciphers subordinated to the demands of the role of Manfred. We are always aware of the inevitability of ultimate nonvolition on the part of Manfred after Astarte herself has refused to be moved toward him by the volition either to condemn or to forgive.

The quality of the protagonist is perhaps not quite so apparent in the third canto of *Childe Harold's Pilgrimage,* a poem revealing its own structural integrity but related to the first two and the last canto of *Childe Harold* only by title and some rather feeble attempts of the speaker to confirm the relation. The speaker fails in this, just as he fails to sustain the image of the title character, Harold. It has long been taken as a weakness in the poem itself that the character of Harold is dropped and the "I" of the speaker assumes the principal role for approximately the last half of the poem. Read as a simple, direct confessional poem, the third canto of *Childe Harold's Pilgrimage* would seem to justify the usual suggestion that Byron merely became tired of the device of Harold and abandoned it. I have found reason, however, which I shall endeavor to present in one of the following essays, to read the poem in another way. The speaker would consciously make Harold his projection (some would call it an alter ego), a means by which he, the speaker, would simply purge his feelings and the pain of his quest for an emotionally unified view of the world by transferring these to Harold. But he fails. In the Rhine Journey, which is the architectonic *and* the psychological center of the third canto of *Childe Harold,* the speaker abandons Harold. Thereafter every section of the poem, in which the speaker is concerned with his own isolation and failure, echoes a section before the Rhine Journey, in which he was supposedly concerned with the imaginary Harold's isolation and failure. The result is that the structure of the poem reveals a nonmechanical symmetry of which the Rhine Journey is obviously the center and the opening and closing addresses by the speaker to his daughter are the bounds. The second half of the poem mirrors the first half, and the total poem possesses organic wholeness rather than merely an accidental sequence of personal passages.

Within the second group of protagonists I should principally place those of the poems *The Prisoner of Chillon, The
Lament of Tasso, Mazeppa,* and perhaps with some qualifications *The Prophecy of Dante.* Called by various names, these
are all dramatic monologues. In these poems, the protagonists
(formerly or presently placed in, respectively, a prison, a
madhouse, defeat in battle, and exile) seek to make over their
individual visions of the world in such a way that they can
find justification for their various plights and sufferings and
thus for further motivation and action. They have perhaps
become, to varying degrees, what today we might call para-
noid, regarding themselves as the objects of both human persecution and providential favor. We as readers are always
aware of the ambiguities of their position, as they exist between the real world of the flesh and the ideal world of either
aspiration or, most obviously in the case of the prisoner of
Chillon and Tasso, delusion.

Byron's plays reveal qualities characteristic of the Middle
Phase, and in at least one instance, *Werner,* the poet failed
in the creation of a distinct, identifiable character, as badly
as he had ever done during the First Phase of his work. From
the time that Byron began to work on *Don Juan,* in which
he used a complex form demanding many of the techniques
characteristic of the dramatic monologue, though he wrote
many other poems, he produced little else of quality. The
later dramas, with the exception of *Cain* and *Heaven and
Earth,* reveal, from almost any point of view, but limited
success. We can only make conjectures concerning the cause.
It is quite apparent that in *Marino Faliero, Sardanapalus,*
and *The Two Foscari,* the poet employed situations which
were significant largely from an interior, rather than an ex-
terior, viewpoint, and that he would have achieved sustaining
irony had he constructed monologues about them; but in
attempting to give external projection to these situations, he

merely directed attention away from those characters centrally involved. In each instance the situation is of such a nature that it can be seen in full perspective only if it is seen ironically, through a juxtaposition of the external and internal positions.

In the following essays, I have not attempted to make an extensive survey of Byron's poetry[20] and have avoided, as much as possible, particular consideration of individual poems as representative of the genres to which they have been traditionally assigned. I have been primarily concerned, of course, with the structure of the poems discussed, regarding some of those of the Middle Period as intrinsically significant and all of those considered as important in the development toward *Don Juan,* particularly the later and more complicated cantos of that poem. It is, in the whole sense of my work, with this development to the level and nature of the achievement in *Don Juan* that I have been concerned rather than with *Don Juan* itself, to the structure of which I have devoted only my concluding remarks.

II

English Bards and
Childe Harold, I and *II*

BOTH *English Bards and Scotch Reviewers* AND *Childe Harold's Pilgrimage,* Cantos I and II, appears to be constructed after established models, the Popean and the Spenserian, and for this reason these poems have been taken by many to represent, respectively, Byron's "early classicism" and his departure into "romanticism." The generalization usually passes unchallenged, but analysis of the poems themselves offers somewhat less than full support of it. Examination does reveal at least that the poems have this point in common, that perhaps more than any other of Byron's major works they leave the critic little of a positive nature with which to deal—in narrative, symbol, or irony—so that he is inevitably and consistently forced into the quest for the biographical correlative, which can be a beginning but hardly become an end. Despite the outer support given each poem by the facts of its origins and genre, neither *English Bards and Scotch Reviewers* nor the first *Childe Harold* reveals a sustained structure, either intellectual or dramatic.

i

English Bards and Scotch Reviewers appears to be essentially a series of sketches which have little inner relation

27

other than the fact that each concerns a literary or historical figure. Such is not entirely the case, for the speaker (in this instance one not distinct from the poet) attempts, for conventional purposes, to imply the nature of the ideal and the one by describing explicitly the real and the many. That he fails to do so may be ultimately, and perhaps rather obviously, attributed to that Byronic incapacity, already described, to conceive of other than a fragmentary universe, so that the antithesis which should sustain the structure of the poem collapses. A symptom of collapse and thereby a more immediate cause for failure is the overemphasis of the multiplicity of bad bards and reviewers. Despite the quality that is apparent in some short passages, the poem is not sustained in its length, which becomes thereby excessive. The structural failure can best be understood perhaps in terms of Byron's use but final abandonment of a metaphor that should become the cohesive force in the poem, the traditional equation between priest and poet. Described simply, the speaker's employment of this metaphor is incomplete, never passing beyond the proposition that the bards and reviewers "in these degenerate days" are not priestlike, as others once were. He points to Pope and Dryden as historical ideals; but in describing the lesser bards of the contemporary scene, the speaker does not reveal, by ironic implication or otherwise, the nature of the quality of the older poets.

In the first 102 lines of *English Bards and Scotch Reviewers* (those passages preceding the opening of the earlier *British Bards*), the speaker establishes the need for his poem. He now takes up once more "Nature's noblest gift—my grey goose-quill" (line 7), which he has laid aside. His call is not merely to write, however, for that would only add one more to the number of minor writers already abroad. Rather, it is to hold up to ridicule the follies of these authors and thereby to reaffirm the nobility of the pen: "I'll publish, right or wrong: / Fools are my theme, let Satire be my song" (5-6). He becomes at once, therefore, the instrument of a higher need. In the second stanza the speaker develops the contrast between himself and other writers. His own quill, "Slave of my thoughts, obedient to my will," compares with that of any lesser bard, "*Torn* from thy *parent* bird to form a pen, / That mighty instrument of little men" (8-10; italics mine). The Caesarean image anticipates the picture which follows, of related kinds of unnatural birth:

> The pen! foredoomed to aid the mental throes
> Of brains that labour, big with Verse and Prose;
> Though Nymphs forsake, and Critics may deride,
> The Lover's solace, and the Author's pride
>
> (11-14)

Prolific but soon forgotten, the pens of others are unlike his, "mine own especial pen," which, its task completed, shall once more be laid aside, "Though spurned by others, yet beloved by me" (19-22). The following stanza establishes the simple functional distinction between good and evil: "Folly, frequent harbinger of crime," is restrained from reaching conclusions only by satire, for "E'en . . . the boldest" will "shrink from Ridicule, though not from Law" (27-36). In the fourth stanza the speaker admits his own limitations as the agent of satire: "The royal vices of our age demand / A keener weapon, and a mightier hand" (39-40)—an admission which suggests the abundance if not the stature of those whom he would attack. Thereafter he sketches the qualities necessary for contemporary critics, who are, by the next stanza, easily described as the "usurpers on the Throne of Taste" (84). Since they do rule, however, the speaker necessarily concludes that the similarity of "all modern worthies" renders it "doubtful whom to seek, or whom to shun; / Nor know we when to spare, or where to strike, / Our Bards and Censors are so much alike" (89-92). In the concluding stanza oi the introductory section, the speaker, rejecting what he regards as the modern critics' insistence on mechanical regularity in their adaptation of Popean irregularity, proposes the central juxtaposition in the poem: "Better to err with Pope, than shine with Pye" (102). Implicit in lines 89 to 92, the statement prepares for the poet-priest metaphor.

Beginning with a pun, the metaphor is sustained by allusions to the English Reformation. The speaker, recalling the time "ere yet in these degenerate days / Ignoble themes obtained mistaken praise" (103-4), plays upon the name of the eighteenth-century poetic prototype:

> Then, in this happy Isle, a Pope's pure strain
> Sought the rapt soul to charm, nor sought in vain;
> A polished nation's praise aspired to charm,
> And raised the people's, as the poet's fame
>
> (109-12)

The fact that Pope was Catholic contributes to the force of the pun, especially since Dryden, a late convert to Catholicism, is then named Pope's peer; the references following, to Congreve and Otway, dissipate the force of the allusion, but the suggestion remains concerning the nature of what has befallen the Catholic view, in Taste as well as in Church. In the place of the one standard, accepted as true but permitting the irregularity attributed to a Pope or a Dryden ("For Nature then an English audience felt" [116]), there are the many which are false, expressed by the bards whose works are both too numerous and essentially mechanical: "Southey's Epics cram the creaking shelves, / And Little's Lyrics shine in hot-pressed twelves"—some among the "varied wonders" of the age (127-31):

Nor less new schools of Poetry arise,
Where dull pretenders grapple for the prize:
O'er Taste awhile these Pseudo-bards prevail;
Each country Book-club bows the knee to Baal,
And, hurling lawful Genius from the throne,
Erects a shrine and idol of its own;
Some leaden calf—but whom it matters not,
From soaring Southey, down to groveling Stott
(135-42)

The speaker then refers to several among the multiplicity of genres that appear on the contemporary literary scene, showing special concern with Scott and emphasizing the mercenary motive: "Let such forego the *poet's sacred name,* / Who rack their brains for lucre, not for fame" (177-78; italics mine). The poet-priest metaphor, which has been implicit up to this point, is soon made clear:

These are the themes that claim our plaudits now;
These are the Bards to whom the Muse must bow;
While Milton, Dryden, Pope, alike forgot,
Resign their hallowed Bays to Walter Scott
(185-88)

It is sustained by recurring allusion through nearly four hundred lines, to the point at which the speaker turns to the recital of the roll of the many dramatists whose work constitutes the "motley sight" in front of him (560).

To the speaker Southey, a false priest, becomes, in his *Joan of Arc*, a worker of false miracles:

To him let Camoëns, Milton, Tasso yield,
Whose annual strains, like armies, take the field.
First in the ranks see Joan of Arc advance,
The scourge of England and the boast of France!

> Though burnt by wicked Bedford for a witch,
> Behold her statue placed in Glory's niche;
> Her fetters burst, and just released from prison,
> A virgin Phoenix from her ashes risen
>
> (203-10)

Moving somewhat lower in the hierarchy, the speaker describes Wordsworth, "the dull disciple of thy [Southey's] school, / That mild apostate from poetic rule" (235-36), whose lack of standards imposes upon his poetic records of man the impression of a total disorganization of experience. Coleridge, a still lesser figure, is idolatrous, "The bard who soars to elegize an ass" (262). M. G. Lewis, "Monk, or Bard, / Who fain would make Parnassus a church-yard," is merely "Apollo's sexton" rather than his priest, at best perhaps the priest of death: "wreaths of yew, not laurel, bind thy brow" (265-68). Thomas Moore ("Little! young Catullus of his day") emerges as the priest of lust,

> Who in soft guise, surrounded by a choir
> Of virgins melting, not to Vesta's fire,
> With sparkling eyes, and cheek by passion flushed
> Strikes his wild lyre, whilst listening dames are hushed
>
> (283-87)

The metaphor is not present in the lines concerned with the translator Viscount Strangford and the miscellaneous writer William Hayley (295-318) but is then resumed:

> Moravians, rise! bestow some meet reward
> On dull devotion—Lo! the Sabbath Bard,
> Sepulchral Grahame, pours his notes sublime
> In mangled prose, nor e'en aspires to rhyme;
> Breaks into blank the Gospel of St. Luke,
> And boldly pilfers from the Pentateuch;

And, undisturbed by conscientious qualms,
Perverts the Prophets, and purloins the Psalms
(319-26)

The opening reference, though ironic, recalls the earlier allusion to the Reformation, and James Grahame becomes for the speaker a literal instance of a bad priest pretending to be a poet.[1] This example is followed at once by another, that of William Lisle Bowles ("Thou first, great oracle of tender souls"), whose indiscriminately exercised "Sympathy" fosters a multiplicity, "A thousand visions of a thousand things," at once evidence of the breakdown of a central imposing unity in Bowles's world view (327-32). Ultimately the speaker urges Bowles, "Stick to thy Sonnets, Man"; or if he must do otherwise, he should attempt to understand Pope where other critics have failed (362-84).

Following his attack upon Amos Cottle (385-410), the speaker turns briefly toward Thomas Maurice and James Montgomery, both of whom had been attacked by the *Edinburgh Review*. He then centers upon the Scotch reviewers ("Northern Wolves, that still in darkness prowl; / A coward Brood, which mangle as they prey, / By hellish instinct, all that cross their way" [429-31]), especially "immortal Jeffrey," to whom now he twice offers a mock pledge (438, 460). The second of these introduces a brief, ironic account of the duel between Jeffrey and Thomas Moore,[2] in which "Caledonia's goddess hovered o'er / The field, and saved him from the wrath of Moore" (490-91). In a long speech the deity ordains Jeffrey: "Resign the pistol and resume the pen; / O'er politics and poesy preside, / Boast of thy country, and Britannia's guide" (499-501), concluding at length, "the kilted Goddess kist / Her son, and vanished in a Scottish mist" (526-27).

In the discussion of the contemporary theater and its

world, which follows (560-686), the poet-priest metaphor would appear to have no functional part, except by implication, since those whom the speaker discusses are false poets and therefore false priests; from two denials he can hardly derive a positive proposition.

In the next section of the poem, the speaker invokes Truth to "rouse some genuine Bard, and guide his hand / To drive this pestilence from out the land" (687-88). Somewhat later, he promises once more to lay aside his own pen "when some Bard in virtue strong, / Gifford perchance, shall raise the chastening song" (701-2). The speaker then considers the multiplicity of instances of literary error, "the smaller fry, who swarm in shoals" (707)—the Peers, political hacks, and tradesmen who write—before he pays the tribute due to Campbell and Rogers, whom he explicitly makes, in his direct address to them, the priests of Apollo:

> Arise! let blest remembrance still inspire,
> And strike to wonted tones thy hallowed lyre;
> Restore Apollo to his vacant throne,
> Assert thy country's honour and thine own.
> What! must deserted Poesy still weep
> Where her last hopes with pious Cowper sleep?
> (805-10)

Gifford slumbers and is urged to awaken. Henry Kirk White died in full promise. Invention now passes for Genius and Truth, and there are few who, like Walter Wright, have pressed to Greece, the place "Where dwelt the Muses at their natal hour" and prelapsarian poets:

> Wright! 'twas thy happy lot at once to view
> Those shores of glory, and to sing them too;
> And sure no common Muse inspired thy pen
> To hail the land of Gods and Godlike men
> (867-80)

The speaker then calls upon the translators, "who snatched to light / Those gems too long withheld from modern sight," now to "Resign Achaia's lyre, and strike your own" (881-90). It is "these, or such as these," the actual or potential priests of Apollo, who must "Restore the Muse's violated laws," rather than such false poets as Erasmus Darwin and Wordsworth (891-910).

In an address to Walter Scott, the speaker recalls those whom he has previously damned at much greater length, then concludes:

> Let Stott, Carlisle, Matilda, and the rest
> Of Grub Street, and of Grosvenor Place the best,
> Scrawl on, 'till death release us from the strain,
> Or Common Sense assert her rights again;
> But Thou, with powers that mock the aid of praise,
> Should'st leave to humbler Bards ignoble lays:
> Thy country's voice, the voice of all the Nine,
> Demand a hallowed harp—that harp is thine
>
> (927-34)

"Common Sense" must be taken in its earlier, rather than in any modern, sense, becoming thereby the single standard, that of Pope and others, which prevailed before the false Reformation that the speaker has completely rejected. Yet another survey of the present scene dampens the speaker's spirit. "What avails the sanguine Poet's hope, / To conquer ages, and with time to cope?" he asks, and at length concludes that modern Britain has become the "dark asylum of a Vandal race! / At once the boast of learning, and disgrace!" (949-90). He repeats that he, "thus unasked," has attempted "to tell / My country, what her sons should know too well"; and with an expression of the hope that somehow Britain's Bards may "rise more worthy" of Britain's name, the speaker concludes what was the earlier poem, *British Bards* (991-1010). The closing passages in the present poem are more directly personal than those preceding, containing the speaker's (here most clearly the poet's) reiteration of his intentions and then his farewell as he prepares to journey forth. Like the long section devoted to the contemporary drama and various short passages in which the poet abandons what he has apparently made the cohesive metaphor in *English Bards and Scotch Reviewers,* the concluding lines severely weaken the structure of the poem.

ii

Childe Harold's Pilgrimage comprises essentially three poems—Cantos I and II; Canto III; Canto IV—each composed and published at a different stage of Byron's career but all held together by a common title and, in the minds of most readers, by a rather heavy wrapping of biographical allusion.

A reading of the first poem, the first two cantos of *Childe Harold,* may be externally conditioned by three factors: the title, the Preface, and the epigraph. Though these elements impose upon the poem much of the meaning it has, ultimately they serve to emphasize how little structural cohesiveness the poem possesses.

The fact is often overlooked that the title specifies that the poem is about a "Pilgrimage," and that the poem is subtitled *A Romaunt.* Within the tradition, the protagonist of the verse romance is sent upon a mission, the fulfillment of which will prove his courage and other qualities needed for moral survival; the end of the pilgrimage must be the test itself. In the Preface to *Childe Harold, I* and *II,* however, the poet qualifies the direction that the title seems to give to the poem. The work is primarily descriptive, he proposes, "written, for the most part, amidst the scenes which it attempts to describe"; but in order to give "some connection to the piece," structural cohesiveness, he has introduced a protagonist, who, he implies, must not be taken too seriously for what the title suggests he is: "It is almost superfluous to mention that the appellation 'Childe,' as 'Childe Waters,' 'Childe Childers,' etc., is used as more consonant with the old structure of versification which I have adopted." Form rather than structural potential becomes dominant, therefore, in directing the poet toward his material.

The assertion expressed through the title remains before us, however, though its aesthetic force has been significantly weakened; the object of the pilgrimage is still justifiably a consideration. The epigraph, taken from Fougeret de Monbron's *Le Cosmopolite, ou, le Citoyen du Monde* (1753), proposes:

L'univers est une espèce de livre, dont on n'a lu que la première page quand on n'a vu que son pays. J'en ai feuilleté un assez grand nombre, que j'ai trouvé également mauvaises. Cet examen ne m'a point été infructueux. Je haïssais ma patrie. Toutes les impertinences des peuples divers, parmi lesquels j'ai vécu, m'ont réconcilié avec elle. Quand je n'aurais tiré d'autre bénéfice de mes voyages que celui-là, je n'en regretterais ni les frais ni les fatigues.

The passage suggests that in the poem that follows the protagonist's quest is to be primarily social. In the early lines of the first canto of *Childe Harold,* however, it is made explicit that the basis for affirmation which Harold has lost and would regain is either psychological or metaphysical rather than merely social.

The first canto closes with the statement that Harold is still "doomed to go" onward (I, xciii). As a character he supposedly becomes "the gloomy Wanderer o'er the wave" (II, xvi). The frame of the poem—the quest of the Hero, his

Night Journey—suggests the possibility of irony developing within the poem itself: the Hero would appear to seek that which for him can have no being, so that the poem becomes a kind of inverted romance. But in the first two cantos of *Childe Harold* such promise fails in fulfillment, primarily because the protagonist himself does not emerge. He is introspective to the degree that, from an external viewpoint, he appears unmotivated. Whatever has disillusioned him has no apparent relation to anything beyond the Self to which he would direct action or thought: it is given no significant dramatic projection. Harold is essentially fleeing rather than searching; he seeks only to escape. But escape, as a motivation, need not remain merely negative, if that which one seeks to escape is of emotional (and therefore of dramatic) significance. In Harold's case it is guilt, "For he through Sin's long labyrinth had run" (I, v), but his guilt never becomes more than the object of description, essentially passive. The reason for this may be, quite simply, that *if* Harold is motivated, as a character he never really moves. He begins as an observer of mankind, a result of course of the central fact of isolation, but neither consciously nor outwardly does he develop from this point, so that what he sees—the death of the bull, viewed as either ritual or sport, is an example—causes no credible reaction in him. A split becomes obvious between the force of the descriptions of scenes through which Harold passes and the limited degree to which these affect him. This, which might seem to be an inevitable and consistent result of his own fragmented world view is in fact an immediate result of the fragmentary nature of the narrative structure of the poem. Within the frame of Harold's travels, narrated as they are by a third person, there is no dramatic tension. This might have been at least established by the elementary device of protagonist-antagonist conflict; or by the more complex instrument of dramatic irony, achieved by the juxtaposition in the speaker of the conscious and unconscious levels of expression, by which the potential offered by the split described above could be realized.

But there is none of this. The first two cantos of *Childe Harold's Pilgrimage* do not essentially pass far beyond that point at which they begin, that of "descriptive poetry"; and the phrase itself, if it is taken to mean poetry that describes without the use of symbolic or dramatic structures, is self-contradictory. At best the method of the poem is only narrative when the supposed subject, Harold as a complex personality, demands that it become dramatic.

III

The Early Tales

THE EARLY TALES ARE CONSTRUCTED PRIMARILY THROUGH THE interaction of the elementary themes of Love and Death. In the simpler of the Tales, the principal characters tend, in varying degrees, to assume allegorical dimensions, largely representing either Love, Death, or a fusion of both; in the more complex Tales, the characters no longer serve primarily the single, self-evident demands made by the narrative but move toward the achievement of dramatic intensity through the obvious juxtaposition of their conscious and unconscious beings. Of the first type *The Bride of Abydos* and *The Corsair* are examples. *Lara* and *The Siege of Corinth*, read in context as personal recollections by their respective speakers, illustrate the transition to the second type, of which *Parisina* (completed shortly after, but published with, *The Siege of Corinth*)[1] represents the full development.

i

The narrative of *The Bride of Abydos* is almost entirely concerned with action, represented from a viewpoint that is not discernibly that of one who has known the actors. They themselves are limited to four (Selim, Zuleika, Giaffir, and Haroun), who seem to respond simply and directly to stimuli and to move on only one plane of existence. Because of this simplicity and the closeness of the relation among the characters, an overt pattern can be seen in the interaction of the two motifs, which is in turn reflected by the symbols emerging from the setting.

In *The Bride of Abydos* the story is quite simple. Selim, whom we first regard as the son of Giaffir, is in love with his supposed half-sister, Zuleika. He suffers the contempt of Giaffir, who considers Selim sufficiently unmanly to be permitted to possess a key to the harem. Selim soon reveals to Zuleika that he is not, in fact, her half-brother but her cousin, for his own father was the brother of Giaffir, whom the latter murdered. Living apart from the court, Selim has become the leader of a pirate band, by which means he has satisfied his need for freedom and action as much as his hatred for Giaffir. In consideration of Zuleika's feelings, Selim promises that when the time arrives for him to strike, he will spare Giaffir. Lingering in the place of rendezvous with Zuleika, however, Selim is set upon by Giaffir's soldiers; hesitating in his retreat so that he might gaze once more at Zuleika, Selim is killed. Zuleika has already died of heartbreak, leaving Giaffir to avenging solitude.

According to the parts played in the action, it becomes rather apparent that, viewed in terms of the two dominant motifs in the poem, Zuleika is the Love figure and Giaffir the Death figure. The first canto is clearly the Love canto, the second the Death canto; the guise of Selim appears to be the key. Selim represents the antithesis of Death and of Love in turn, and in the second canto, by his association with Zuleika, the potential for the resolution of the conflict of these motifs through union. Haroun, the eunuch, though frequently the instrument for Love or Death, becomes a clear instance of intrinsic failure in dealing with both. Of the four characters he alone has no choice between them. Giaffir persistently chooses Death or Death giving, Zuleika Love or Love giving, and Selim reacts to the nature of the principal whom he faces.

The elements of the opening setting become in part suggestive of the antithetical forces in the action. Specifically, "the cypress and myrtle / Are emblems of deeds that are done in their clime." "The rage of the vulture, the love of the turtle" oppose but become fused, and the melancholy nightingale sings eternally where the winds blow fragrantly over the rose gardens. Such is the background, where "all, save the spirit of man, is divine" (I, 1-19). Giaffir emerges at once, a pointed dramatization of Man's spiritual darkness, whose every motive and means of judging Life itself are expressed in terms of Death. Described as "old" and with "aged eye," he is unconquerably proud: "His pensive cheek and pondering brow / Did more than he was wont avow" (I, 20-31). Clearing the hall of all except Selim, Giaffir, significantly using a Death image, orders Haroun to bring Zuleika "from her tower" so that he might announce her betrothal: "Her fate is fixed this very hour." Selim stands "at the Pacha's feet: / For son of Moslem must expire, / Ere dare to sit before his sire!" The struggle between generations, implicit in the rivalry of Selim and the aged fiancé which Giaffir is about to bestow upon Zuleika, is simply expressive of the thematic dichotomy in the poem. Selim now admits that, unable to sleep in the early morning ("let the old and weary sleep"), he broke in upon Zuleika's sleep in the harem. Then together, "Before the guardian slaves awoke / We to the *cypress* groves had flown" (italics mine), where, he recalls, they lingered long, telling the story of Mejnoun and Leila, star-crossed lovers,

> Till I, who heard the deep tambour
> Beat thy Divan's approaching hour,
> To thee, and to my duty true,
> Warned by the sound, to greet thee flew:
> But there Zuleika wanders yet—
> Nay, Father, rage not—nor forget
> That none can pierce that secret bower
> But those who watch the women's tower
> (I, 32-80)

Though Giaffir is angry, it is because of Selim's apparent unmanliness rather than the possibility of an amorous relationship between Selim and Zuleika. In Giaffir's view, though Selim should be concerned with the bow and the steed, he "Greek in soul if not in creed, / Must pore where babbling waters flow, / And watch unfolding roses blow" (I, 87-89). From this view Giaffir derives certitude regarding Zuleika's security with Selim, for Giaffir measures Love-making power by Death-making power, therefore giving Selim the same freedom of the harem that he allows Haroun:

> I mark thee—and I know thee too;
> But there be deeds thou dar'st not do:
> But if thy beard had manlier length,
> And if thy hand had skill and strength,
> I'd joy to see thee break a lance,
> Albeit against my own perchance
>
> (I, 120-25)

Giaffir, darkly hinting at Selim's origins, reveals his own essential insecurity: "I would not trust that look or tone: / No —nor the blood so near my own" (I, 139-40). For his part, Selim silently harbors thoughts of revenge.

Only Zuleika brings forth anything resembling positive impulses from Giaffir:

> Zuleika came—and Giaffir felt
> His purpose half within him melt:
> Not that against her fancied weal
> His heart though stern could ever feel;
> Affection chained her to that heart;
> Ambition tore the links apart
>
> (I, 187-92)

He addresses her, intentionally anticipating her marriage but ironically foretelling her Death through Love:

> Zuleika! child of Gentleness!
>   How dear this very day must tell,
>   When I forget my own distress,
>   In losing what I love so well,
>   To bid thee with another dwell
>   (I, 193-97)

Again, he judges Love power by Death power, unknowingly thereby referring to Selim rather than to Zuleika's fiancé: "Another! and a braver man / Was never seen in battle's van" (I, 198-99). Zuleika's intended husband is "kinsman of the Bey Oglou," an old man, with whom marriage would become for Zuleika another kind of Death through Love. "I would not have thee wed a boy," Giaffir remarks. He promises "a noble dower" and sufficient strength from the union of their two powers to "teach the [enemy] messenger what fate / The bearer of such boon may wait." His use of "fate" is crucial, recalling his earlier anticipation of Zuleika's marriage, the significance of which he now measures entirely in terms of its subsequent Death-giving capacity. Such is his, a father's, will: "All that thy sex hath need to know: / 'Twas mine to teach obedience still— / The way to love, thy Lord may show" (I, 205-18). Silently Zuleika hears her "fate," and Giaffir goes forth to scimitar practice, his "game of mimic slaughter" (I, 219-52).

Alone with Selim, Zuleika promises that her Love for him will not permit her to leave him and will, in fact, even transcend Death:

> Ev'n Azrael, from his deadly quiver
>   When flies that shaft, and fly it must,
> That parts all else, shall doom for ever
>   Our hearts to undivided dust!
>   (I, 323-26)

In her ironic prophecy she has equated her father, the one who is to kill Selim, with the Angel of Death. Her avowal of Love restores Selim to awareness, as is emphasized in a series of images of Death dealing:

> A war-horse at the trumpet's sound,
> A lion roused by heedless hound,
> A tyrant waked to sudden strife
> By graze of ill-directed knife,
> Starts not to more convulsive life
> Than he, who heard that vow, displayed,
> And all, before repressed, betrayed
>   (I, 340-46)

Selim affirms his own Love for Zuleika, recalls Giaffir's reproaches, and in the cause of Love promises to become a Death giver:

>   to none be told
> Our oath; the rest shall time unfold.
> To me and mine leave Osman Bey!
> I've partisans for Peril's day:
> Think not I am what I appear;
> I've arms—and friends—and vengeance near
>   (I, 377-82)

Ironically, however, Selim, who has appeared to Giaffir soft and powerless, now seems to Zuleika "sadly changed: / This morn I saw thee gentlest—dearest— / But now thou'rt from thyself estranged" (I, 384-86). His Love has made him appear Deathlike to the Love figure. She attempts to quiet him, by reaffirming her Love for him and mentioning those obligations it imposes upon her—all things, she remarks (again with unknowing, ironic prophecy), "but close thy dying eye, / For that I could not live to try" (I, 404-5). She then asks Selim the reason for "so much of mystery"; when they have seen the Trochadar preceding Giaffir returning from the mimic war, Selim promises to meet her after sunset and reveal "My tale, my purpose, and my fear: / I am not, love! what I appear" (I, 408-82).

The first canto opened with Giaffir, before whom Selim appeared soft and effeminate; in the opening of the second, Zuleika, going to the grotto which has always symbolized to her peace and revery, finds arms piled high and Selim himself dressed as a Death maker:

> His robe of pride was thrown aside,
>   His brow no high-crowned turban bore,
> But in its stead a shawl of red,
>   Wreathed lightly round, his temples wore:
> That dagger, on whose hilt the gem
> Were worthy of a diadem,
> No longer glittered at his waist,
> Where pistols unadorned were braced;
> And from his belt a sabre swung,
> And from his shoulder loosely hung
> The cloak of white, the thin capote
> That decks the wandering Candiote;
> Beneath—his golden plated vest
> Clung like a cuirass to his breast;
> The greaves below his knee that wound
> With silvery scales were sheathed and bound.
> But were it not that high command
> Spake in his eye, and tone, and hand,
> All that a careless eye could see
> In him was some young Galiongée
>
>   (II, 613-32)

Selim soon reveals to Zuleika that he is not her brother, and she, who has known nothing other than this relationship as the basis for their Love, immediately assumes the opposite of Love in his present intentions: "If thou hast cause for vengeance, see! / My breast is offered—take thy fill! / Far better with the dead to be / Than live thus nothing now to thee." The breast, with which she has expressed the idea of Death, is most frequently a Love symbol. Selim protests that he is moved only by Love, then with unconscious irony foretells: "Thy lot shall yet be linked with mine." He hates her father, for a relationship usually bound by Love ("My father was to Giaffir all / That Selim late was deemed to thee") was terminated when Giaffir killed his own brother. Selim, however, promises "no present vengeance" against Zuleika's father. Strangely, where Death giving would be expected, Giaffir pitied and spared the infant Selim, who was then raised "as a son / By him whom Heaven accorded none." Only Haroun, the former servant of Selim's father, knows the full story, for he (who could not save his master because presumably he had no Death power as he had no Love power) brought the child to Giaffir at a time when the tyrant was inclined to mercy (II, 647-729).

Selim continues his tale, recalling that, prevented by Giaffir's fears from learning the arts of war at home "And taunted to a wish to roam," he became "leader of those pirate hordes, / Whose laws and lives are on their swords" (II, 785-844). The ambiguity of his position is now fully apparent. He now proposes the fusion of the forces of Love and Death, by their union, the only way possible: "But be the Star that guides the wanderer, Thou! / Thou, my Zuleika, share and bless my bark; / The Dove of peace and promise to mine art!" (II, 877-79) Selim, the Death figure to others, promises to become the Love bringer to Zuleika:

> Girt by my band, Zuleika at my side,
> The spoil of nations shall bedeck my bride.
> The Haram's languid years of listless ease

Are well resigned for cares—for joys like these:
Not blind to *Fate,* I see, where'er I rove,
Unnumbered perils,—but one only love!
Yet well my toils shall that fond *breast* repay,
Though Fortune frown, or falser friends betray
                    (II, 894-901; italics mine)

Selim anticipates escaping "with the favouring gale, / Which Love to-night hath promised to my sail" (II, 930-31). He promises that her Love will cause him to spare her father, but that, if necessary, by his own Death he would prevent her marriage to the Osman (II, 950-72).

At the point of full hope, however, the lovers are set upon by the forces of Giaffir. Selim fights, "His pistol's echo rang on high," but Zuleika, unable to comprehend the forces of Death, "started not, nor wept, / Despair benumbed her breast and eye!" Seeing his boat and band, Selim strikes forth amid "A swarming circle of his foes," through whom he fights his way. About to leave the shore and move toward his men, Selim turns to look for Zuleika: "That pause, that fatal gaze he took, / Hath doomed his death, or fixed his chain." A ball fired by Giaffir finds its mark; Love, Selim's final motivation, has brought Death (II, 973-1058).

On the following morning Nature offers only Death symbols: "The sea-birds shriek above the prey, / O'er which their hungry beaks delay." The Osman Prince, Zuleika's betrothed, arrives, but "is come too late," for Zuleika is dead. The reference to her "virgin grave" brings together both motifs and recalls "the cypress and myrtle" of the opening of the poem. Giaffir, to whom Zuleika was the only object of Love, has (by acting out his very nature and expressing his Love for her by sending Death to Selim) brought Death to her. "Woe to thee, rash and unrelenting Chief!" the narrator intones,

Vainly thou heap'st the dust upon thy head,
Vainly the sackcloth o'er thy limbs dost spread:
By that same hand Abdallah [Selim's father]—Selim bled.
Now let it tear thy beard in idle grief:
Thy pride of heart, thy bride for Osman's bed,
She, whom thy Sultan had but seen to wed,
        Thy Daughter's dead!
Hope of thine age, thy twilight's lonely beam,
The Star hath set that shone on Helle's stream.
What quenched its ray?—the blood that thou hast shed!
Hark! to the hurried question of Despair:
'Where is my child?'—an Echo answers—'Where?'
                                    (II, 1065-1145)

In "the place of thousand tombs," only "The sad but living cypress glooms / And withers not," though stricken "with an eternal grief, / Like early unrequited Love" (II, 1146-51). There is no myrtle. Yet one spot bears a rose, to which "A Bird unseen—but not remote" sings a "note so piercing and profound" that to some it seems to "shape and syllable its sound / Into Zuleika's name" (II, 1146-94). A monument placed one evening where Zuleika lies was found next morning where Selim fell, and there, it is said, at night appears "a ghastly turbaned head, so that the monument is now called the "Pirate-phantom's pillow." The rose, the "mourning flower," lives still, "Alone and dewy—coldly pure and pale; / As weeping Beauty's cheek [reflecting Love] at Sorrow's tale [of Death]!" (II, 1195-1214).

Despite major structural similarities between *The Bride of Abydos* and *The Corsair,* the character of the protagonist in the later work is developed slightly beyond those of the principals in *The Bride of Abydos.* The duple structure of *The Corsair* derives largely from the opposition between the two motifs, Love and Death, in the being of Conrad himself. For him Love is associated with Woman, Death with Man. The first canto, dominated by the image of Medora in the setting of their island retreat, is the Love canto; the second, in which Conrad attacks the Seyd, is clearly that of Death; and the third, in which Gulnare (moved by Love for Conrad as well as hatred for the Seyd) destroys her lord and Medora dies of Love, contains the fusion of both. The work is given episodic unity by the theme of the quest, which is brought to culmination not in Conrad's destructive venture against the Seyd but in his ultimate return to Medora's dark tower. Here he faces the problem of reconciling Love and Death, which has been intensified because Gulnare (a Woman, therefore a Love symbol) has brought Death to the Seyd. Medora's own Death for Love, psychologically fulfilling for Conrad the demands of his myth, appears to achieve for him the necessary reconciliation.

ii

Lara might be regarded by some, the author suggested in his Advertisement, "as a sequel to the *Corsair;*—the colouring is of a similar cast, and although the situations of the characters are changed, the stories are in some measure connected. The countenance is nearly the same—but with a different expression." Byron appears to have written very little elsewhere about *Lara*.[2] The result has been what is perhaps a consistent misreading of the tale or at least a failure to grasp hints concerning the one fact in the narrative which gives it some form of structural unity.

In the story, Lara returns to his ancestral domain, followed by only the loyal page Kaled. At the festival of his neighbor Otho, Lara is apparently recognized as a former outlaw by Sir Ezzelin, who threatens to reveal Lara's supposed crimes.

Ezzelin and Lara promise to meet the following day at Otho's to settle their difficulties, but Ezzelin never arrives. After a struggle with Otho, who has guaranteed the appearance of Ezzelin, Lara becomes an outcast from his class, leads a revolt of the serfs, is wounded in battle, and dies. Following Lara's death, it is discovered that Kaled is a woman. The next scene emerges from the retelling of the tale of a serf who saw an unidentified horseman put into the river between Otho's and Lara's lands a form that appeared by its clothing to be the body of Ezzelin. Broken by grief, Kaled remains fixed at the spot of Lara's death until she herself dies.

From the beginning those few critics who have concerned themselves with *Lara* have either openly accepted the fact or at least implied that Lara was Ezzelin's murderer.[3] The matter is related to any judgment of the structure of the poem, for so long as Lara is assumed to be the murderer, the Ezzelin element and the Kaled element within the plot are related only by the person of Lara, so that following the death of Lara, both the discovery of Kaled's sex and the peasant's revelation of the method used to dispose of Ezzelin's body become anticlimactic. The assumption of Lara's guilt seems to underly the rather standard view of the poem, that "the interest . . . lies not in the story but in the character of Lara, in which one may see the author's conception of himself."[4] Since the character of Lara is contrived beyond the limits of credibility, the critic is frequently forced to depend largely or entirely upon biographical correlation in order to make positive assertions about the poem,[5] but in themselves these do not lead toward judgments of the work. Thus, though suggesting a firmer relation between the Ezzelin and Kaled elements will not eliminate many of the weaknesses in the poem, it will reveal a source for unity of structure that *Lara* has not previously appeared to possess. The only basis for such a relation between these elements is the hypothesis that, within the action of the story, it appears to be Kaled rather than Lara who kills Sir Ezzelin.

So far, however, stating the hypothesis in this way seems only to beg the question. Evidence supporting it must be found in the poet's work rather than in the critic's need. Externally the question of the relation of this poem to *The Corsair* becomes significant, for if *Lara* is a sequel, as the poet implied it might be, then Lara is clearly Conrad and Kaled is Gulnare;[6] at least part, then, of what both recall is Gulnare's vindictive murder of the Seyd and Conrad's subsequent reaction to it:

> He had seen battle—he had brooded lone
> O'er promised pangs to sentenced Guilt foreshown;
> He had been tempted—chastened—and the chain
> Yet on his arms might ever there remain:
> But ne'er from strife—captivity—remorse—
> From all his feelings in their inmost force—
> So thrilled, so shuddered every creeping vein,
> As now they froze before that purple stain.
> That spot of blood, that light but guilty streak,
> Had banished all the beauty from her cheek!
> Blood he had viewed—could view unmoved—but then
> It flowed in combat, or was shed by men!
> *(The Corsair, III, 1586-97)*

If Lara, after promising that he will appear to face Ezzelin's charges, is either the instigator or the perpetrator of the murder of Ezzelin, then he has been completely deprived of that respect for honor that is essentially characteristic of Conrad. Such inconsistency would not be demonstrated if Kaled were the murderer, for her code (necessarily the Oriental code of Gulnare) would in no way forbid her secret destruction of one who threatened him she loved.

But again, these assertions, concerning matters that are

essentially extrinsic to the poem, appear to beg the question. The characters in *Lara,* moreover, as they may be derived from those in *The Corsair, need not* demonstrate consistency. A suggestion that is useful may come from any source, but a hypothesis can be sustained only by what is in the poem itself. A close reading of certain passages of *Lara,* particularly as they qualify one another by anticipation or recollection, strengthens the suggestion, and perhaps moves far in sustaining the view, that Kaled kills Ezzelin.

The frame of the tale is dramatic, for the story comes to us largely through a speaker, who, though not obtrusive, is the interpreter of much of the action. He is irregular in his use of tenses, moving by emotional rather than intellectual force from the present to the past and back again. On occasion he appears to answer himself or one to whom he is presumably telling the story: "Why did she love him? Curious fool!—be still— / Is human love the growth of human will?" (II, 1175-76). Explicitly identifying himself as one of the witnesses to Lara's death and by implication therefore one of Otho's band ("But from his [Lara's] visage little could we guess" [II, 1107]), the speaker sees and reports most events from a position external to the characters, though he interposes comment and conjecture upon what he sees: after telling how Kaled "flung back" the Crucifix proffered to Lara shortly before death, the speaker remarks that Kaled "Nor seemed to know his [Lara's] but *then* began— / That Life of Immortality, secure / To none, save them whose faith in Christ is sure" (II, 1132-34). The speaker, essentially simple and occasionally superficial, discerns few, if any, of the implications in the action that he recounts; in fact, even the way in which he has put his story together reveal aspects of it which, in terms of his apparent conclusions, he would seem to be unaware. It is this speaker, in this instance totally distinguished from the author, who, retelling the peasant's tale of the disposal of the body of Ezzelin, attempts to interpret the incident and in "charity" expresses the hope that Lara was not Ezzelin's murderer, thereby arousing and directing suspicion that such was the case. It is of course undeniable that the poet has been inconsistent in his use of a speaker, so that at times authorial revelation seems to become confused with that of the speaker, and the essential structure of the poem is thereby weakened;[7] but failure to recognize the distinction between author and speaker, which operates through much of the work, has perhaps caused misreading and a somewhat unjust estimate of the poem.

In the first canto of *Lara,* containing the rising action of the narrative, the center of interest broadens from the protagonist to the association between Lara and his page. In the long passage concerning Kaled (I, 528-623), the speaker consciously anticipates the discovery of Kaled's sex and at the same time unknowingly implies a basis for her motivation to kill Ezzelin. Its function is, therefore, structurally dramatic rather than, as the speaker himself would seem to believe, merely atmospheric.

The opening stanzas contain the speaker's account of Lara's return. He was "seared by toil, and something touched by Time" (I, 56) and accompanied by "No train . . . beyond a single page" (I, 47). Though remote, evading "long questions of the past" (I, 85), Lara was warmly welcomed "to the haunts of men," where "still he only saw, and did not share, / The common pleasure or the general care" (I, 96-102). His own world contained solitary study and contemplation, offering at least substance for the conjecture of his vassals: "Why slept he not when others were at rest? / Why heard no music, and received no guest? / All was not well, they deemed—but where the wrong?" (I, 147-49) During one of his nocturnal wanderings, beset by either an enemy or a strange fit, Lara was found by those of the household, "Cold as the marble where his length was laid, / Pale as the beam that o'er his features played." Near him lay "his half-drawn sabre," and on his brow was evidence of defiance: "Though mixed with terror, senseless as he lay, / There lived upon his lip the wish to slay" (I, 211-18). Slowly he came to consciousness, speaking a language that was meaningless to all around him. It is at this point, a moment of crisis of which the meaning is veiled to all others, that the page emerges as a character; though the speaker would appear to be unaware of the implications, Lara's situation becomes a device by which to heighten attention upon the page, who

> approached, and he alone appeared
> To know the import of the words they heard;
> And, by the changes of his cheek and brow,
> They were not such as Lara should avow,
> Nor he interpret,—yet with less surprise
> Than those around their Chieftain's state he eyes,
> But Lara's prostrate form he bent beside,
> And in that tongue which seemed his own replied;
> And Lara heeds those tones that gently seem
> To soothe away the horrors of his dream—
> If dream it were, that thus could overthrow
> A breast that needed not ideal woe
>
> (I, 235-46)

In the speaker's account of the incident there is the faint (and certainly unconscious) suggestion that the page, who had presumably become aware by this time of the nature of Lara's "wish to slay," took upon himself the evil that afflicted his master. Lara came forth the following day with "new vigour in his shaken frame," the speaker remarks and then adds disapprovingly, "And solace sought he none from priest nor leech" (I, 250-51).

In time, Lara (who possessed "an art / Of fixing memory on

another's heart" [I, 363-64]) accepted an invitation to Otho's Festival, at which, remaining detached from the group, he was soon made the object of Ezzelin's mysterious accusations: "Thou *shunn'st* no question! Ponder—is there none / Thy heart must answer, though thine ear would shun? / And deem'st thou me unknown too? Gaze again!" (I, 437-39). Lara refused to listen, but Otho interposed to suggest that they meet on the following day to hear Ezzelin's charges. "I pledge myself for thee, as not unknown," he remarked to Ezzelin, adding with some emphasis:

> And if from Lara's blood and gentle birth
> I augur right of courage and of worth,
> He will not that untainted line belie,
> Nor aught that Knighthood may accord, deny
>
> (I, 464-77)

The question of the truth in Otho's assumption is of course vital. Lara appears to have been moved by feelings of social isolation rather than of moral guilt, and there has been, in the speaker's account of Lara's detachment from men, no implicit suggestion that he violated the code supposedly distinguishing his class from others. That in time Lara was to oppose that class in rebellion does not essentially alter his attitude toward its code and obligations therein.[8] That Lara, unlike Ezzelin, accepted Otho's terms only after prolonged silence (during which "to its centre shrunk / His soul, in deep abstraction sudden sunk" [I, 482-83]) can be taken as evidence either that he was contemplating the seriousness of the pledge or that he was contriving a means of avoiding the obligation that the promise would impose.

Following his assent, "further word / Than those repeated none from Lara heard." The speaker reports seeing no indication of Lara's emotional reaction. "Yet there was something fixed in that low tone," he recalls, "Which showed resolve, determined, though unknown" (I, 490-95). Then passing Ezzelin, Lara smiled ("Could this mean peace? the calmness of the good? / Or guilt grown old in desperate hardihood?" the speaker wonders) and "called his page, and went his way" (I, 496-510). Presumably the speaker consciously intends at this point to anticipate Lara's murder of Ezzelin, but the facts of Lara's behavior, regarded in their position in the speaker's narrative, may lead elsewhere. It is perhaps significant not merely that the joint departure of Lara and his page precedes that of Ezzelin (I, 624-27) but that the intervening lines direct attention toward the page. It is the reaction of the page to the ominous hints in Lara's expression and tone, which ironically the speaker himself appears unable to discern, rather than the reaction of the speaker that may be crucial. If this is the case, then Lara's smile at Ezzelin becomes a motivating element within the dramatic structure of the poem rather than a decorative appendage to the characterization of Lara. It is primarily a cause rather than an effect, but a principal characteristic of the speaker, from which arises the somewhat limited irony in the poem, is his extreme awareness of effect but limited perception of cause.

The transition to the passage describing the page makes clear the point that he was Lara's "only follower" and Lara his only guide (I, 512, 526). Verbal communication between them was in the page's language. The page himself was unlike others in his age and station, the speaker reports: "For hours on Lara he would fix his glance, / As all-forgotten in that watchful trance." Otherwise he was solitary and "seemed, like him he served, to live apart / From all that lures the eye, and fills the heart" (I, 528-53). Hence, if he loved any, " 'twas Lara," as he showed clearly "in deeds alone; / In mute attention," and (a fact, like the two preceding, perhaps far more significant than the speaker, here consciously anticipating the discovery of the page's sex, could suspect) in "care, which guessed / Each wish, fulfilled it ere the tongue expressed" (I, 554-57). Aloof from the "familiar crew" and seemingly "Of higher birth," the page possessed a hand "So femininely white it might bespeak / Another sex, when matched with that smooth cheek," except for

> his garb, and something in his gaze,
> More wild and high than Woman's eye betrays;
> A latent fierceness that far more became
> His fiery climate than his tender frame:
> True, in his words it broke not from his breast,
> But from his aspect might be more than guessed
> (I, 571-83)

His name was Kaled, "though rumor said he bore / Another ere he left his mountain shore," for on occasion he failed to answer to the name (I, 584-91).

The descriptive phase of this passage prepares for the account of Kaled's reaction to the incident in Otho's hall. The speaker again recounts this as effect, therefore as an added commentary (by Kaled in this instance) on Lara's character rather than as an indication of Kaled's own growing intentions with respect to Ezzelin. The speaker appears to fail, in other words, to recall his own remark of a moment ago, that Lara's expression seemed to the page to anticipate verbal command. Kaled, who had seen the strife in the hall from above, learned from the crowd the nature of the incident:

> The colour of young Kaled went and came,
> The lip of ashes, and the cheek of flame;
> And o'er his brow the dampening heart-drops threw
> The sickening iciness of that cold dew,
> That rises as the busy bosom sinks
> With heavy thoughts from which Reflection shrinks.

Yes—there be things which we must dream and dare,
And execute ere thought be half aware:
Whate'er might Kaled's be, it was enow
To seal his lip, but agonise his brow.
He gazed on Ezzelin till Lara cast
That sidelong smile upon the knight he past;
When Kaled saw that smile his visage fell,
As if on something recognised right well:
His memory read in such a meaning more
Than Lara's aspect unto others wore:
Forward he sprung—a moment, both were gone,
And all within that hall seemed left alone

(I, 598-615)

The principal question posed by these lines concerns *what*
Kaled remembered (if indeed the speaker's conjecture is
correct that Kaled remembered anything). At first this might
seem to be an act by Lara, but (even apart from any consideration of the poem as a sequel to *The Corsair*) after it becomes
known that Kaled was a woman, suspicion must be directed
toward Kaled herself as much as toward Lara. The speaker
ponders sleep and death (I, 628-45), and the canto closes.

The speaker's description of the coming of morning opens
the second canto. By noon the nobles had assembled in Otho's
hall, but Ezzelin was absent. Otho reaffirmed his pledge. Lara
insisted upon the absurdity of Ezzelin's charges: "I know him
not—but me it seems he knew / In lands where—but I must
not trifle too: / Produce this babbler—or redeem the pledge."
Otho of course accepted "the last alternative," and in the
ensuing struggle fell but would not beg for life. Lara, on the
point of killing Otho, was restrained by the crowd of nobles,
who "thus for mercy dared to interpose." Lara's break with
his peers thus became complete. He left the hall, allowing
Otho to recover as well as he could (II, 674-733).

The speaker is soon concerned with the disappearance of

Ezzelin, with particular emphasis on his friends' quest for recognizable clues. That they found none suggested to them the unfamiliar and gave them further reason to cast suspicion toward Lara. In time Otho recovered and, "a man of power and Lara's foe," demanded that justice seek "Account of Ezzelin at Lara's hands," arguing from the position that a motive had been established:

> Who else than Lara could have cause to fear
> His presence? who had made him disappear,
> If not the man on whom his menaced charge
> Had sate too deeply were he left at large?
> (II, 772-81)

Linked with "The general rumour ignorantly loud, / The mystery dearest to the curious crowd" and the human tendency "rather to condemn than praise," Otho's view in time prevailed to raise a cry against Lara (II, 782-801). Meanwhile, always the friend of the oppressed, Lara had extended his political activities, even freeing his own serfs, so that "when Otho thought / Secure at last the vengeance which he sought," he discovered "the destined criminal / Begirt by thousands in his swarming hall" (II, 857-60). From that moment, Lara, raising "the humble but to bend the proud" (II, 898), was rebellion's leader.

The "tale of strife" is passed over quickly: early victory yielded to "blind confusion," the effects of "The lust of booty, and the thirst of hate," and finally to discontent: "Lara's soul alone seems still unbent" (II, 909-64). Finally, "Commanding —aiding—animating all," Lara was struck and quickly removed from the field by Kaled. Otho and his forces came upon the dying Lara and stood silently by as Lara and Kaled spoke in "that other tongue." "They seemed even then—that twain—unto the last / To half forget the present in the past," the speaker remarks, "To share between themselves some separate fate, / Whose darkness none beside should penetrate." Offered the Cross, Lara "looked . . . with an eye profane," but Kaled, "With brow repulsive, and with gesture swift, / Flung back the hand which held the sacred gift" (II, 1013-1134).

Following Lara's death, Kaled fainted, and those trying to revive the page discovered her sex. In the telling of his story, the speaker has reached a point of intensity, the revelation of "The secret long and yet but half concealed" (II, 1160), which he has artfully tried to anticipate in his narration. Within the larger structure of the poem, however, it is perhaps a moment of achieved dramatic irony simply because the speaker fails to realize that as a woman Kaled would have the double motive to destroy Ezzelin arising from her love for Lara and her aversion to discovery. The speaker shifts quickly to a description of Lara's grave, made at the spot where he died. Kaled's "quiet grief" foretells her own death: "But that wild tale she brooked not to unfold, / And sealed is now each lip that could have told" (II, 1183-84). But at this point the speaker interjects the peasant's tale, which, in the light of knowledge of Kaled's origin and sex, may assume significance that would not otherwise be apparent.

A serf abroad before sunrise, passing near the river dividing "Otho's lands and Lara's broad domain," saw a horseman emerging from the woods: "before him was a cloak / Wrapt round some burthen at his saddle-bow, / Bent was his head, and hidden was his brow." Curious, the serf watched as the figure "reached the river, bounded from his horse, / And lifting thence the burthen which he bore, / Heaved up the bank, and dashed it from the shore." Furtively he looked about, apparently alarmed lest "even yet too much its surface showed," then found stones and cast them at the floating mass until it sank. Though the "face was masked" so that "the features of the dead, / If dead it were," escaped the serf's view and possible recognition, he saw on the breast a star, "the badge that Knighthood ever wore, / And such 'tis known Sir Ezzelin had worn / Upon the night that led to such a morn." The horseman waited until the last eddy had ebbed, then quickly departed. His method of disposal of the dead, "If dead it were," is reminiscent of the supposedly Oriental, but to the speaker, retelling the serf's tale, only the obvious meaning comes: characteristically he prays for Ezzelin, "If thus he perished, Heaven receive his soul! / His undiscovered limbs to ocean roll." And with "charity" the speaker hopes that "It was not Lara's hand by which he fell" (II, 1195-1242).

In the final passage of the second canto, resembling in its contemplativeness the last lines of the first, the speaker tells of Kaled's death. Fixed to a spot near Lara's grave, she in time became deranged. Her mind seemed to be entirely concerned with Lara. She tried to stanch "some phantom wound," presumably Lara's though perhaps Ezzelin's as well. She assumed Lara's part as well as her own in an imaginary dialogue, again appearing to take upon herself the evil afflicting her master, "Then, rising, start, and beckon him to fly / From some imagined Spectre in pursuit." In time her fit exhausted her, and she died. "Her tale untold," the speaker concludes.

iii

The relatively slight critical consideration given *Parisina* has been primarily concerned with the question of the poet's failure to bring moral judgment to the work. If this is the criterion, then he failed indeed, for (despite E. H. Coleridge's assertion that "the *dénouement* of the story is severely moral")[9] the poet offers neither comment nor implication regarding the good or evil of the actions of the characters. Instead, he presents an essentially dramatic situation, of which the psychological aspects are inescapable.[10]

Azo, the Marquis of Este, married to the beautiful Parisina, is the father, by a youthful affair with Bianca, of Hugo; he discovers that Hugo, a former suitor of Parisina, has become her lover, and he condemns his son to death and his wife to a punishment of which the nature is never revealed. The development and indeed the strength of the work arise principally from the nature of the relationship, both conscious and unconscious, among these three persons, especially as it is expressed in the tension between father and son.

The poem opens with the central situation. In the evening Parisina and Hugo meet, but in time they leave "The spot of guilty gladness past" (50), Hugo going "to his lonely bed" (65) and Parisina to her place beside Azo. By simple displacement at a critical moment the sleeping Parisina murmurs Hugo's name. For Azo "the shock" is intensified because Hugo, the former suitor, is "the child of one / He loved" (101-2) and therefore the personification of what sense of guilt Azo might have and a constant reminder of his loss of Bianca; presumably the birth of Hugo ("The offspring of his wayward youth, / When he betrayed Bianca's truth") terminated Azo's affair with Bianca ("The maid whose folly could confide / In him who made her not his bride"), so that Hugo has become the object of Azo's projection, "his own all-evil son" (102-6).

After resisting the immediate impulse to destroy Parisina in her sleep, Azo goes forth the following morning to seek "The proof of all he feared to know, / Their present guilt." Consciously he regards this as the cause of "his future woe," since it will deprive him forever of Parisina, but he has unconsciously seized upon the situation as the instrument, in fact the excuse, for the removal of Hugo. "The long-conniving damsels" among Parisina's attendants save themselves and satisfy the demands of what appears to be repressed resentment of their lady by a familiar process: they "would transfer / The guilt—the shame—the doom—to her." Their accusations establish for Azo as fact the possibility which, though consciously torturing him, unconsciously gratifies his need for a seemingly rational basis for his attribution of his own sense of guilt to Hugo. He immediately has the lovers arraigned before him.

The persons of the court, like the attendant ladies, who have formerly shown only respect for Parisina, now regard the fallen Marchioness, "With downcast eyes, and knitting brow, / And folded arms, and freezing air, / And lips that scarce their scorn forbear" (163-65): jealousy can now be rationalized in the name of loyalty to the Marquis and to the code of morality. Hugo remains proud, seemingly unmoved by sorrow, though, we are told, he dared not look at Parisina, "Else had his rising heart betrayed / Remorse for all the wreck it made" (196-97). But mixed with Hugo's conscious grief at Parisina's plight is an unconscious satisfaction at the pain which he has caused Azo, who, he feels, has wronged him by transferring to him his own image of guilt.

Azo's opening words are ironic: "But yesterday / I gloried in a wife and son: / That dream this morning passed away" (198-200). He has never regarded Hugo in what is traditionally the light of a son, but now, forced to act as judge, Azo assumes the character of the injured but duty-bound father. He protests, perhaps overmuch, that he is acting as he should, that *their* guilt offers him no alternative:

> My life must linger on alone;
> Well,—let that pass,—there breathes not one
> Who would not do as I have done:
> Those ties are broken—not by me;
> Let that too pass;—the doom's prepared!
> (202-6)

And thereby he rationalizes his real but repressed desire to destroy Hugo. The pattern of projection is quite clear as Azo urges Hugo to do exactly what, within the bounds of his own religious belief, he himself should feel compelled to do: go to the waiting priest, "address thy prayers to Heaven; / Before its evening stars are met, / Learn if thou there canst be forgiven" (209-11). But, instead, Azo seeks to remove his own guilt by destroying its embodiment. His well-established feelings toward his son, now justified by the moral trespass of the lovers, become perfectly apparent to us, though not to him, in his self-righteous pronouncement: "But here, upon the earth beneath, / There is no spot where thou and I / Together for an hour could breathe" (213-15). Driven, however, by an unreconciled (and indeed unrecognized) sense of his present guilt, Azo refuses to watch Hugo's execution, insisting that Parisina do what he cannot: "But thou, frail thing! shalt view his head." He is unable, he protests, "to speak the rest." At once he falls back upon rationalization, both of his general action toward the lovers and of the specific ordeal just imposed upon Parisina: "Go! woman of the wanton breast; / Not I, but thou his blood dost shed" (217-20).

Hugo requests and receives permission to speak. Addressed to Azo, the words of Hugo constitute a rather remarkable analysis of those motives of which he has become conscious in his act against his father and at the same time a clear revelation of the processes which are still at work in his mind below the level of the conscious. He must first associate himself with his father:

> It is not that I dread the death—
> For thou hast seen me by thy side
> All redly through the battle ride,
> And that [Hugo's sword]—not once a useless brand—
> Thy slaves have wrested from my hand
> Hath shed more blood in cause of thine,
> Then e'er can stain the axe of mine
>
> (234-40)

Hugo's assumption of the possession of the axe, the instrument to be used in his execution, is the means by which he symbolizes the completion of his victory over his father, his revenge for what he feels is the cause of the death of his mother and for his own humiliation, which can end only in his own death.[11] This process of identification of the axe as his own, and by extension of his father with himself, becomes the basis for a messianic view of himself, by which he sees himself sacrificed not as the agent but as the victim of his father. Unconsciously Hugo appears to be doing the same thing as Azo, in other words, but he is moving in the opposite direction; in the fact of his own death he is projecting toward Azo what guilt he might feel. "Thou gav'st, and may'st resume my breath," he remarks, "A gift for which I thank thee not." At the same time, identifying himself with his father, Hugo unconsciously assumes the place of the father in the reconstructed relationship with Bianca, of which the affair with Parisina has been in part a symbol, a re-enactment:

> Nor are my mother's wrongs forgot;
> Her slighted love and ruined name,
> Her offspring's heritage of shame;
> But she is in the grave, where he,
> Her son—thy rival—soon shall be
> (241-47)

He has been his father's "rival" in two senses, of which that relating to his mother appears to be primary: Parisina has, at a less than conscious level, come to assume for Hugo the place of mother as well as step-mother. Now, with conscious irony, Hugo insists upon Azo's guilt: Bianca's "broken heart" and his own "severed head" shall serve as witnesses "from the dead / How trusty and how tender were / Thy youthful love —paternal care" (248-51).

Following an apparent admission of guilt (" 'Tis true that I have done thee wrong"), which is at once qualified by an expression of satisfaction ("But wrong for wrong"), the utterances of Hugo become somewhat broken:

> this,—deemed thy bride,
> The other victim of thy pride,—
> Thou know'st for me was destined long;
> Thou saw'st, and coveted'st her charms;
> And with thy very crime—my birth
> Thou taunted'st me—as little worth;
> A match ignoble for her arms;
> Because, forsooth, I could not claim
> The lawful heirship of thy name,
> Nor sit on Este's lineal throne
>
> (252-62)

There are two possible readings of the passage. The word "this" could refer to the *fact* of the "wrong" that he has committed against his father, which, he still feels, has long been his due; the interpolation would seem to refer to Bianca and become part of the structure of Hugo's justification. Then it is Bianca's "charms" of which he now speaks, and in the following couplet Hugo again points to the results of Azo's affair with Bianca—his own birth and wretched position, which have rendered him unfit, "ignoble," for Parisina. The word "this" could just as easily refer to the *essence* of the "wrong" which Hugo has committed, that is, the affair with Parisina, which then becomes the subject of the clause "for me was destined long"; Parisina was young and Hugo was aware of her "charms," but these were coveted by Azo, who in turn taunted Hugo with his illegitimacy and declared him "a match ignoble for her arms." The problem of identifying Hugo's object of reference, Bianca or Parisina, is unreal, for in his vengeance upon his father Hugo has unconsciously made Parisina the substitute for Bianca (he has in fact fused the two), so that in his fragmentary utterance characterizing his emotional state, there is no clear antecedent for the word "her" modifying "charms." The weight of logic might incline us toward Parisina perhaps, but with regard to the speaker this is hardly a factor.

Hugo now remarks that despite his exclusion from claim to the throne, within "a few short summers" he would have proved himself no more "ignoble" than legitimate princes: "My name should more than Este's shine / With honours all my own." His "sword" would have become his instrument, a "crest" the symbol of his success. He finds the basis for rationalization in history, which reveals to him that "Not always knightly spurs are worn / The brightest by the better born," and in recollection of his own valor in the service of Este and of his father (263-75). His subsequent identification of himself and his father,

> Yet in my lineaments they trace
> Some features of my father's face,
> And in my spirit—all of thee.
> From thee this tamelessness of heart—
> From thee—nay, wherefore dost thou start?—
> From thee in all their vigour came
> My arm of strength, my soul of flame—
> Thou didst not give me life alone,
> But all that made me more thine own
>
> (285-93)

intensifies the earlier suggestion (234-40) and permits him to insist upon his inner nobility ("I am no bastard in my soul" [296]) and consequently upon the injustice of Azo's persecution of him. Beneath the level of the conscious, however, the identification also enables Hugo to intensify his fusion of Parisina and Bianca, his projection toward Azo of what guilt he might feel, and his sense of vengeance upon his father: "See what thy guilty love hath done! / Repaid thee with too like a son!" (294-95).

Recalling once more that his father and he "all side by side, have striven, / And o'er the dead our coursers driven" (302-3), Hugo suggests that death in battle at that earlier time would have been preferable to the death that he must now face:

> For though thou work'dst my mother's ill,
> And made thy own my destined bride,
> I feel thou art my father still:
> And harsh as sounds thy hard decree,
> 'Tis not unjust, although from thee.
> Begot in sin, to die in shame,
> My life begun and ends the same:
> As erred the sire, so erred the son,
> And thou must punish both in one.
> My crime seems worst to human view,
> But God must judge between us two!
>   (307-17)

The opening five lines of the passage would appear to be merely a conscious expression of repentance: despite the injury which Azo caused by his affair with Bianca and despite the fact that Azo rather than his son married Parisina, Hugo senses his kinship with Azo and is sorry for the wrong that he has committed. That these lines also express an instance of reversal of what is really Hugo's unconscious satisfaction at the deep unhappiness that he attributes, perhaps by projection, to his father becomes rather clear in the lines which follow, beginning "Begot in sin, to die in shame"; here, continuing the earlier identification of himself with his father, Hugo gives final expression to his introjection, appearing to take upon himself his father's sin in begetting him, so that he might conclusively insist upon projection, transferring his own guilt with Parisina to his father. Hugo's less-than-conscious purpose comes quite close to the surface in his concluding utterance, that though his "crime" may seem worse than Azo's to man, "God must judge" as well as man. But even at this point the word "crime" is ambiguous, for, as should now be quite apparent, Hugo has been, from the beginning, acting out and then rationalizing his lifelong hatred of his father.

Following the close of Hugo's speech, Parisina falls into a state of shock, repressing the details of her experience:

> She feared—she felt that something ill
> Lay on her soul, so deep and chill;
> That there was sin and shame she knew,
> That some one was to die—but who?
> She had forgotten
>
> (368-72)

Hugo is executed, messianically refusing the binder for his eyes: "These hands are chained, but let me die / At least with unshackled eye— / Strike" (450-52). And amid the horrified sighs of all who watch, there comes from Azo's palace "a woman's shriek—and ne'er / In madlier accents rose despair" (498-99).[12] Thereafter Parisina is not "heard or seen," and her name is "banished from each lip and ear, / Like words of wantonness or fear" (502-7). Azo himself finds "another bride" and becomes the father of "goodly sons" (530-31), but he seems to live without emotional response, suppressing any outward show of conscious grief, which appears to veil a much deeper sense of pain or guilt:

> The deepest ice which ever froze
> Can only o'er the surface close;
> The living stream lies quick below,
> And flows, and cannot cease to flow.

Still was his sealed-up bosom haunted
By thoughts which Nature hath implanted;
Too deeply rooted thence to vanish,
Howe'er our stifled tears we banish;
When struggling as they rise to start,
We check those waters of the heart,
They are not dried—those tears unshed
But flow back to the fountain head,
And resting in their spring more pure,
For ever in its depth endure,
Unseen—unwept—but uncongealed,
And cherished most where least revealed
(553-68)

By his subsequent marriage Azo attempted "to fill again /
The desert gap which made his pain." Attributing guilt to
Hugo and Parisina, he lived "Without the hope to meet them
where / United souls shall gladness share." The fault, he
persistently affirmed, was theirs ("they had wrought their
doom of ill") rather than his, for "he / Had only passed a just
decree." Beneath the level of conscious affirmation, however,
he remained unpersuaded: "Azo's age was wretched still"
(571-78).

IV

Childe Harold, III, and *The Prisoner of Chillon*

i

THE THIRD CANTO OF *Childe Harold's Pilgrimage* HAS BEEN adversely judged on occasion because Byron does not sustain Harold as the central character but, instead, allows the "I" of the poem to usurp Harold's position. Despite the rather apparent fact that the poem lacks the degree of cohesiveness found in the monologues and certain other poems of the later periods, there is reason to attribute greater organization to the poem than this estimate suggests.

The poem may be regarded as a dramatic utterance. The speaker, having failed to achieve interior resolution of his problem, attempts to project it; he strives to create a dream world, in which Harold, the image of the Self or the alter ego, is to assume and dramatize (thereby possibly resolving into harmony) the emotional elements disturbing the speaker. That the speaker is unable to do this simply gives dramatic emphasis to the essential fact that he himself has not found emotional resolution and that, in his conscious attempts to reconstruct a meaningful system of belief out of his experiences, he has not escaped the limits of the Self. Ironically, the failure of the speaker to sustain the image of Harold strengthens rather than weakens the poem.

Isolation, the principal theme of *Childe Harold, III,* is

dramatized by the speaker's apostrophe to his daughter, with which the poem opens and to which he returns as he approaches conclusion:

> Is thy face like thy mother's, my fair child!
> Ada! sole daughter of my house and heart?
> When last I saw thy young blue eyes they smiled,
> And then we parted,—not as now we part,
> But with a hope.—
> Awaking with a start,
> The waters heave around me; and on high
> The winds lift up their voices: I depart,
> Whither I know not; but the hour's gone by,
> When Albion's lessening shores could grieve or glad mine eye
> (III, i)

> My daughter! with thy name this song begun!
> My daughter! with thy name thus much shall end!—
> I see thee not—I hear thee not—but none
> Can be so wrapt in thee; Thou art the Friend
> To whom the shadows of far years extend:
> Albeit my brow thou never should'st behold,
> My voice shall with thy future visions blend,
> And reach into thy heart,—when mine is cold,—
> A token and a tone, even from thy father's mould
> (III, cxv)

Few have failed to notice the general unity that this device imposes upon the poem, but most have found little evidence beyond this of structural cohesion. The highly personal quality of the utterances obviously renders the speaker's isolation emotionally more credible; moreover, it emphasizes that despite his attempts to project, even to universalize, his isolation (thereby, ironically, destroying it by sharing it), he retains it necessarily as an element of the Self as it was in the beginning. Within this framework the elements of the speaker's attempted projection, though they clearly do not form a mechanical unit, follow an organic pattern, which rises to its high point in the stanzas devoted to the Rhine Journey.

The speaker is alone ("Once more upon the waters! yet once more! / And the waves bound beneath me as a steed / That knows his rider"), in a situation in which he necessarily remains passive: "Still must I on; for I am as a weed, / Flung from the rock, on Ocean's foam to sail / Where'er the surge may sweep, the tempest's breath prevails" (III, ii). His one act as poet is necessarily imaginative, to call forth the figure of Harold, "The wandering outlaw of his own dark mind," of whom he sang in youth, "And bear it with me, as the rushing wind / Bears the cloud onwards." He must assume that the figure is truly passive, that he can inform it and make it thereby the object of meaningful projection:

> in that Tale I find
> The furrows of long thought, and dried-up tears,
> Which, ebbing, leave a sterile track behind,
> O'er which all heavily the journeying years
> Plod the last sands of life,—where not a flower appears
> (III, iii)

Necessarily the speaker explicitly establishes the condition of the figure (he has "grown agèd in this world of woe, / In deeds, not years, piercing the depths of life, / So that no wonder waits him"), since Harold himself never actually moves. The speaker attributes to the figure an understanding of the poetic process, by which the figure itself is sustained: he knows "Why Thought seeks refuge in lone caves, yet rife / With airy images, and shapes which dwell / Still unimpaired, though old, in the Soul's haunted cell" (III, v), the speaker asserts:

> 'Tis to create, and in creating live
> A being more intense that we endow
> With form our fancy, gaining as we give
> The life we image, even as I do now.

The image of Harold of course presupposes the consciousness of the speaker, the "I" of the poem, but at the same time it appears to offer it the means of self-transcendence:

> What am I? Nothing: but not so art thou,
> Soul of my thought! with whom I traverse earth,
> Invisible but gazing, as I glow
> Mixed with thy spirit, blended with thy birth,
> And feeling still with thee in my crushed feelings' dearth
>
> (III, vi)

The speaker hesitates: "Yet I must think less wildly." He has in the past "thought / Too long and darkly" until the brain itself has become "In its own eddy boiling and o'erwrought / A whirling gulf of phantasy and flame." He recognizes, however, the essential irreversibility of the process of alienation: " 'Tis too late: / Yet am I changed; though still enough the same / In strength to bear what Time can not abate" (vii).

Dramatic projection rather than introspection, the transcendence rather than the analysis of the Self, offers the only possible means to resolution. "Long absent Harold," therefore, "re-appears at last" (viii) and at once assumes the qualities which the speaker has just attributed to himself: his "enchanted cup" of Life "had been quaffed too quickly, and he found / The dregs were wormwood" (ix), and "soon he knew himself the most unfit / Of men to herd with Man, with whom he held / Little in common" (xii). Hence, like the speaker of course, he becomes an exile, thereby accepting and dramatizing his isolation; yet he nec-

essarily pursues the course of introspection which the speaker
has attempted to supplant with dramatic projection:

> Self-exiled Harold wanders forth again,
> With nought of Hope left, but with less of gloom;
> The very knowledge that he lived in vain,
> That all was over on this side the tomb,
> Had made Despair a smilingness assume,
> Which, though 'twere wild,—as on the plundered wreck
> When mariners would madly meet their doom
> With draughts intemperate on the sinking deck,—
> Did yet inspire a cheer, which he forbore to check
>
> (xvi)

Harold's emotional transmutation is the full expression of the
speaker's projection. It is insubstantial, however, in no apparent way distinct from the emotional conversion of those
(who are imaged somewhat later by the speaker) left desolate
by Waterloo: "There is a very life in our despair, / Vitality of
poison,—a quick root / Which feeds these deadly branches."
This is the basis for sustaining life but hardly (the speaker,
with perhaps unwitting irony, appears to imply) for achieving
art by sublimation. "Life will suit / Itself to Sorrow's most
detested fruit," he remarks, "Like to the apples on the Dead
Sea's shore, / All ashes to the taste" (xxxiv).

The speaker introduces the Waterloo theme with abrupt-
ness ("Stop!—for thy tread is on an Empire's dust" [xvii]),
immediately making his opening reference to Napoleon ("He
wears the shattered links of the World's broken chain"
[xviii]), to whom he returns at the conclusion of the Waterloo
stanzas:

> There sunk the greatest, nor the worst of men,
> Whose Spirit, antithetically mixed,
> One moment of the mightiest, and again

On little objects with like firmness fixed;
Extreme in all things!

(xxxvi)

The essence of the image of Napoleon, sustained through seven stanzas, is its isolation, which springs from "a fever at the core [of the soul], / Fatal to him who bears, to all who ever bore" (xlii). Among others so afflicted, "the madmen who have made men mad / By their contagion," the speaker places "Conquerors and Kings, / Founders of sects and systems, to whom add / Sophists, Bards, Statesmen" (xliii)—those who embody for the speaker the image of Man in isolation:

He who ascends to mountain-tops, shall find
The loftiest peaks most wrapt in clouds and snow;
He who surpasses or subdues mankind,
Must look down on the hate of those below.
Though high *above* the Sun of Glory glow,
And far *beneath* the Earth and Ocean spread,
Round him are icy rocks, and loudly blow
Contending tempests on his naked head,
And thus reward the toils which to those summits led

(xlv)

The "Conquerors and Kings," the first of these, are generally recalled by the empty castles that dominate both the scene and Harold's mood as he begins his Rhine Journey: "And there they stand, as stands a lofty mind, / Worn, but unstooping to the baser crowd, / All tenantless, save to the crannying Wind" (xlvii). The speaker's final projection of Harold contains Harold's own song, "The castled Crag of Drachenfels," occurring at a point somewhat less than half-way through the poem.[1] Thereafter the speaker quietly assumes Harold's place in his account of the Rhine Journey and the passage through the Alps. The song he sings is no longer dramatic, but is now merely a description of his own emotions rather than a record of Harold's. Clearly he has failed. He approaches Lake Leman, where, still feeling pursued ("There is too much of Man here" [lxviii]), he emphasizes that the derivation of isolation may be from emotional incapacity rather than from denial: "To fly from, need not be to hate, mankind" (lxix), that (as he has implied in the second stanza) one in isolation is essentially passive, the object of forces and circumstances beyond the control of the Self:

> The race of life becomes a hopeless flight
> To those that walk in darkness: on the sea
> The boldest steer but where their ports invite—
> But there are wanderers o'er Eternity
> Whose bark drives on and on, and anchored ne'er shall be
>
> (lxx)

Those who are subsequently to fill for the speaker the image of Man in isolation (recalling "Founders of sects and systems . . . / Sophists, Bards, Statesmen" [xliii]) are first "the self-torturing *sophist,* wild Rousseau" (lxxvii; italics mine), then Voltaire, the "Historian, *bard,* philosopher" (cvi; italics mine), and Gibbon (cvii). The French Revolution was the "fearful monument" to Rousseau "and his compeers," failing mankind but in its example foretelling a more thorough upheaval (lxxxi-lxxxiv). From the contemplation of violence and pain the speaker moves abruptly to that of the silence of the Lake, "which warns me, with its stillness, to forsake / Earth's troubled waters for a purer spring" (lxxxv). Affirmation of the reality of the power and love in Nature appears, for the moment, to the speaker to be positive and ultimate expression of one's isolation:

All Heaven and Earth are still: From the high host
Of stars, to the lulled lake and mountain-coast,
All is concentered in a life intense,
Where not a beam, nor air, nor leaf is lost,
But hath a part of Being, and a sense
Of that which is of all Creator and Defence.

Then stirs the feeling infinite, so felt
In solitude, where we are *least* alone;
A truth, which through our being then doth melt,
And purifies from self: it is a tone,
The soul and source of Music, which makes known
Eternal harmony

(lxxxix-xc)

Though he is aware of the power of universal Love, he cannot participate in it beyond attempting in solitude to reproduce its force through art, but in this he must fail: "as it is, I live and die unheard, / With a most voiceless thought, sheathing it [*one* word of ultimate truth] as a sword" (xcvii). The speaker has reached the dilemma to which the essential division in his nature between intellectual recognition and emotional participation has led him. He cannot move; yet it is Man's nature "to advance or die; / He stands not still, but or decays, or grows / Into a boundless blessing" (ciii). While emotionally dying, he has, it would seem, sought to advance by projecting the Self, primarily in Harold but in the other figures as well and in the elements of Nature (the Rhine and the Alps) around him.

The speaker abruptly recalls the scene of Clarens, "birthplace of deep Love!" (xcix). Rousseau's creative process, in this instance essentially projectional, images that of the speaker:

> 'Twas not for fiction chose Rousseau this spot,
> Peopling it with affections; but he found
> It was the scene which Passion must allot
> To the Mind's purified beings; 'twas the ground
> Where early Love his Psyche's zone unbound,
> And hallowed it with loveliness
>
> (civ)

Since, in the picture of Rousseau as in the image of Harold, the speaker has failed to find a basis for emotional resolution, he pauses only briefly to contemplate Voltaire and Gibbon ("gigantic minds," whose "steep aim / Was, Titan-like, on daring doubts to pile / Thoughts which should call down thunder" [cv]), who, living in both physical and emotional exile, also ultimately failed at fulfillment. Most logically, the speaker now "quit[s] Man's work, again to read / His Maker's, spread around me" (cix); his apostrophe to Italy (cx) marks the end of his journey, and with it resignation though not rest. He approaches the last of his song and, emphasizing his necessarily inescapable isolation, makes explicit the failure that has been implicit in his abandonment of the Harold figment:

> I have not loved the World, nor the World me;
> I have not flattered its ranks breath, nor bowed
> To its idolatries a patient knee,
> Nor coined my cheek to smiles,—nor cried aloud
> In worship of an echo: in the crowd
> They could not deem me one of such—I stood
> Among them, but not of them—in a shroud
> Of thoughts which were not their thoughts, and still could,
> Had I not filed my mind, which thus itself subdued
>
> (cxiii)

In the four stanzas (cxv-cxviii) in which he again apostrophizes his daughter, the speaker concludes.

The organic pattern of the poem (it is clearly not mechanical) may at this point be somewhat more apparent. The Rhine Journey stanzas constitute the center of the poem (xlvi-lxi), during which the speaker abandons the Harold figure. Immediately preceding (xliii-xlv) and following (lxii-lxxv) these stanzas are meditations upon Man's isolation; at next remove from the center there are projections of those in isolation, Napoleon before the Rhine Journey (xxxvi-xlii) and Rousseau, Voltaire, and Gibbon (whose ideas fostered the Revolution out of which Napoleon rose) after it (lxxvi-cix); then, one further step removed are the description of Waterloo, the beginning of Harold's journey (xvii-xxxv), and the apostrophe to Italy, which marks the end of the speaker's journey (cx); the description of Harold's isolation as a projection of the speaker's (ii-xvi) is echoed by the speaker's admission of failure and of his own ultimate isolation (cxi-cxiv); the apostrophe to the speaker's daughter opens (i) and closes (cxv-cxviii) the poem. Diagramed, the structure of the third canto of *Childe Harold's Pilgrimage* might assume the following form:

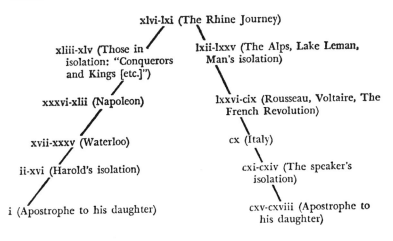

ii

In the usual reading of *The Prisoner of Chillon,* the poem appears to be a record by a man who has conditioned himself to conform to the demands imposed upon him by his immediate surroundings and thereby has overcome adversity. This is the view with which the speaker himself regards his own experience. It has been accepted by most historians, who take to heart Byron's own afterthoughts on the poem presented in a note (now called the "Advertisement"): "When this poem was composed, I was not sufficiently aware of the history of Bonnivard, or I should have endeavoured to dignify the subject by an attempt to celebrate his courage and virtues." Some have apparently accepted the "Sonnet on Chillon" as a reliable comment upon the meaning of the longer poem, but a close examination of *The Prisoner of Chillon* reveals that there is no organic relation between the two poems. That there is the least suggestion of a *meaningful* political theme in the longer poem is simply not the case. Recollection of the "Sonnet," which is concerned primarily with the antithesis between Bonnivard's physical confinement and his intellectual freedom, extrinsically intensifies (as recollection of any similar poem could do) later awareness that in *The Prisoner of Chillon* the protagonist's resolution is ambiguous. Read as a dramatic monologue (as it most frequently is not read), *The Prisoner of Chillon* is the record of a man who, unknowingly, has made over the image of his immediate surroundings to conform to the demands of the Self. Crucial, then, is the nature, rather than the fact, of the intellectual freedom from his material confinement which the speaker in the poem achieves. Emphasis upon the prisoner's interpretation of his own experience should serve only to intensify recognition of the irony of his position rather than to offer a key to the "meaning" of the poem and render it thereby a kind of modern exemplum.

The Prisoner of Chillon begins with the speaker's summary of his experiences and self-sacrifice (i-ii), passes through his account of his life in prison (iii-vi) and the death of his brothers (vii-viii), his description of the bottom of despair (ix) and rediscovery of a world now growing beneficent (x-xiii), and reaches the speaker's resolution (xiv). The longest, and architectonically a central, stanza of the poem, the eighth, contains the *climax* of the speaker's experience (therefore of the poem), though the emotional *crisis* in the story he tells, brought on by the climax, may be more properly assigned to the ninth stanza.[2]

At the opening of the first stanza the speaker makes immediately clear the nature of his view of his own experience: "My hair is grey, but not with years, / Nor grew it white / In a single night, / As men's have grown from sudden fears." He moves from consideration of himself, stressing the duration and intensity of his own sufferings, through description of the confinement and death of his father and brothers, back to the image of himself in isolation. His own survival, which he regards as more than merely physical, becomes the basis for the moral position he now assumes in recounting it:

> We were seven—who now are one,
>   Six in youth, and one in age,
> Finished as they had begun,
>   Proud of Persecution's rage;
> One in fire, and two in field,
> Their belief with blood have sealed,
> Dying as their father died,
> For the God their foes denied;—
> Three were in a dungeon cast,
> Of whom this wreck is left the last.

In his consciousness, as he must attempt to demonstrate in the telling of his tale, the speaker's experience has become essentially allegorical, and he himself has become Man rather than an instance of the Self adjusting its world view to conform with its own demands. If *The Prisoner of Chillon* were the kind of work which many have taken it to be, then in subsequent stanzas there would be, functioning within the dramatic framework of the poem, evidence supporting the speaker's view of his own experience. This is not the case.

In the second stanza the speaker describes the dungeon itself. Implicitly recalling the lines of the first stanza ("My limbs are bowed, though not with toil, / But rusted with a vile repose"), he achieves subjective emphasis primarily by directing attention from the "seven pillars of Gothic mould," to the ring in each, then ultimately to the chain: "That iron is a cankering thing, / For in these limbs its teeth remain, / With marks that will not wear away." In his admission that "this new day / . . . now is painful to these eyes," the speaker appears, at least in conformity with his utterances in the first stanza, to imply that he has received a compensatory insight. As the poem proceeds and he repeatedly reveals his concern with color and tone, however, it becomes apparent that the speaker's loss of visual perspective may not be unrelated to other distortion. The phrase "new day" and those like it occurring through the poem are ambiguous. The speaker concludes this stanza by foretelling the emotional climax of his story (and in so doing suggesting the nature of the structural division in the poem between the more objective first movement [i-viii] and the subjective second [ix-xiv]): "I lost their [the years'] long and heavy score / When my last brother drooped and died, / And I lay living by his side." As in the case of the first stanza, he has concluded with the image of himself in solitude.

In the third stanza, the speaker, essentially repeating what he has already revealed, becomes, for the first time, narrative rather than descriptive: "They chained us each to a column stone, / And we were three—yet, each alone." The action of the first line has been anticipated, and it is only the second which brings full shock. His own emotional stress and that which he would impose upon his story and from which he must derive its meaning is solitude, which he describes first in terms of light: "We could not see each other's face, / But with that pale and livid light / That made us strangers in our sight." Emphasis soon shifts, however, to sound:

> Fettered in hand, but joined in heart,
> 'Twas still some solace in the dearth
> Of the pure elements of earth,
> To hearken to each other's speech,
> And each turn comforter to each
> With some new hope, or legend old,
> Or song heroically bold.

In his story silence is to become an outward sign of his ordeal. The gradual drop in the quality of their voices "to a dreary tone, / An echo of the dungeon stone, / A grating sound," anticipates their death and, of greater significance to the speaker, his own despair following the death of the younger brother. "It might be fancy," the speaker concludes, with ironic qualification, "but to me / They never sounded like our own."

Recalling his brothers and presumably anticipating the moment, within the frame of his narrative, of their death, the speaker makes, at the beginning of the fourth stanza, the most forceful messianic assertion occurring to this point:

> I was the eldest of the three,
>   And to uphold and cheer the rest
>   I ought to do—and did my best—
> And each did well in his degree.

Of his two brothers, the image of the younger is, from the viewpoint of the speaker's present motivation and his interpretation of his experiences, far more significant, emerging first and at far greater length in the speaker's narration in the fourth stanza than that of the elder brother in the fifth. Both serve in recollection as the speaker's objects of comparison with himself, for though they are essentially different from each other, neither (at least as the speaker recalls them) is self-supporting. The younger brother was one "whom my father loved, / Because our mother's brow was given / To him." The speaker's recollection of him creates an image of light (he had "eyes as blue as heaven," was himself "beautiful as day," in fact "a polar day," a "snow-clad offspring of the sun") which forcefully recalls the preceding imagery of light and dark, the "grey" of the speaker's own hair and of the stone, thereby anticipating the degree of despair to which, in the story the speaker tells, the death of this brother is to move the speaker. The bird image ("And truly might it [my soul] be distressed / To see such bird in such a nest"), anticipating the speaker's later reflections upon the bird visiting his prison (which at this point in his narration would be very much in the speaker's mind), is echoed almost at once by the speaker's qualification of his comparison of the younger brother's beauty to that of day ("When day was beautiful to me / As to young eagles, being free"): though in freedom he could be described in terms of external light, in confinement the brother became, without peer, the source of inner light. The implication is consciously psychological rather than theological, though in his judgments the speaker has passed beyond the point at which distinction is possible, and in his present utterance, in fact, he is unconsciously attempting to build a type of theological structure to fulfill psychological needs.

Unlike the younger brother, "With tears for nought but others' ills," the elder of the speaker's two brothers, a huntsman, gives the impression, in the speaker's narrative, of manifest physical strength in freedom. In chains, however, he lacked the inner light:

> His spirit withered with their clank,
>   I saw it silently decline—
>   And so perchance in sooth did mine:
> But yet I forced it on to cheer
> Those relics of a home so dear.

In the speaker's view of himself, made generally clear at the beginning of the fourth stanza, he becomes the necessary complement to each brother: to the one of maternal sympathies he offers a kind of masculine strength, and to him of *once* apparently invulnerable strength he gives understanding. By the end of the fifth stanza the speaker has revealed what is necessary to record the crisis of his experience.

In the sixth stanza he pauses in his narrative to describe the waters of Leman, significantly exaggerated as "A thousand feet in depth below" Chillon's walls. An explicit symbol of life-in-death, the water ("A double dungeon wall and wave / Have made—and like a living grave") became beneficent only in its violence foretelling death:[3]

> We heard it ripple night and day;
>   Sounding o'er our heads it knocked;
> And I have felt the winter's spray
> Wash through the bars when winds were high
> And wanton in the happy sky;
>   And then the very rock hath rocked,
>   And I have felt it shake, unshocked,
> Because I could have smiled to see
> The death that would have set me free.

The suggestion is significant, for as the speaker tells his story (which is essentially about the restoration of the life urge), once more remaking his surroundings that they may conform to his own image of good, the water slowly becomes a symbol that is positive. But rebirth is never final, so that, to some degree, his apparently compulsive telling of his story is unconsciously self-persuasive.

Thus, when, in the seventh stanza, he narrates the death of his "nearer brother," the speaker emphasizes early spiritual decline, for in his own mind he has survived through spiritual strength. For the moment he appears to be digressive, telling of the prison conditions in imagery of the hunt which recalls his earlier description of the elder brother:

> The milk drawn from the mountain goat
> Was changed for water from the moat,
> Our bread was such as captives' tears
> Have moistened many a thousand years,
> Since man first pent his fellow men
> Like brutes within an iron den;
> But what were these to us or him?

The brother's decline, he stresses, was caused by none of these conditions but by confinement itself. "But why delay the truth?" the speaker remarks at length. "He died." In his account of his reaction, the speaker emphasizes the sense of physical isolation which his brother's death intensified: "I saw, and could not hold his head, / Nor reach his dying hand —nor dead." His futile attempts to break his bonds and reach his brother have assumed a significance in the speaker's mind that is apparent only after he tells of the death of the younger brother. Ironically, the older brother achieves in death what the speaker himself just failed to do: "they unlocked his chain, / And scooped for him a shallow grave." The use of "they" is impersonal and becomes more so following the speaker's request, as he now tells his experiences, that the body of his brother be buried in earth that the sun would reach: "They coldly laughed." The present brutality of the keepers intensifies the change that the speaker reports seeing in them after he took the first step, a spontaneous sympathy with the bird (x), leading from the bottom of despair. He must, then, emphasize their cruelty so that ultimately and indirectly he might stress his own spiritual transcendence.

The death of the second brother, which the speaker now recounts (far more slowly than that of the elder of the two), is the climax of the narrative action, which we should distinguish from the emotional crisis in the speaker's experience. Once more he recalls that this brother was "the favourite and the flower" of the family, who soon "withered on the stalk away." After the death of the elder of his brothers, the speaker more clearly assumes the role of father to the younger:

> His mother's image in fair face,
> The infant love of all his race,
> His martyred father's dearest thought,
> My latest care, for whom I sought
> To hoard my life, that his might be
> Less wretched now, and one day free.

All, however, was in vain. "Oh, God!" exclaims the speaker, anticipating the appearance in his narrative of the bird, his principal rebirth symbol, "It is a fearful thing / To see the human soul take wing / In any shape, in any mood." More horrible than other forms of death the speaker had seen, this was "sure and slow." The floral imagery recalls the metaphor at the opening of the stanza: "He faded" gradually, having "all the while a cheek whose bloom / Was as a mockery of the tomb." The speaker unconsciously reveals the cosmic proportions that the passing of his brother assumed for him: "And then the sighs he would suppress / Of fainting Nature's feebleness, / More slowly drawn, grew less and less." In recording the death of his last brother, the speaker emphasizes the emotional rather than the physical aspect of isolation:

> I listened, but I could not hear;
> I called, for I was wild with fear;
> I knew 'twas hopeless, but my dread
> Would not be thus admonishéd;
> I called, and thought I heard a sound—
> I burst my chain with one strong bound,
> And rushed to him:—I found him not,
> *I* only stirred in this black spot,
> *I* only lived, *I* only drew
> The accurséd breath of dungeon-dew.

By his ultimate egoism, the irony in his narrative becomes painfully apparent. He has, in the telling of his story, reached the point at which emerges his central problem, the insistence upon the solution of which is his real, though presumably less than conscious, purpose in the tale:

> The last, the sole, the dearest link
> Between me and the eternal brink,
> Which bound me to my falling race,
> Was broken in this fatal place.

His solitude prepared for the crisis of sanity, which, in his own terms, he now records. He stood on earth deprived of all that he had regarded as the external incentives to continue living. Hereafter, it might seem, his position would necessarily be solipsistic to be at all. In the beginning, therefore, that which one usually attributes to death he found in the Self: "I took that hand which lay so still, / Alas! my own was full as chill." He approached the point of ultimate isolation, of essential despair:

> I had not strength to stir, or strive,
> But felt that I was still alive—
> A frantic feeling, when we know
> That what we love shall ne'er be so.
> I know not why
> I could not die,
> I had no earthly hope—but faith,
> And that forbade a selfish death.

Though he attributes his restraint from suicide to faith, it becomes apparent in what the speaker now records that he soon passed beyond the will to die.

The symptoms recalled in the ninth stanza suggest a type of hysterical paralysis. He loses, first, awareness of light, then sense of space, and (inevitably from this) sense of time. All sense of external reality was erased, and with it, for the moment at least, all affirmation. He fell, as he now reveals, through the levels of animal and vegetable to that of mere matter:

> I had no thought, no feeling—none—
> Among the stones I stood a stone,
> And was, scarce conscious what I wist,
> As shrubless crags within the mist;
> For all was blank, and bleak, and grey;
> It was not night—it was not day;
> It was not even the dungeon-light,
> So hateful to my heavy sight,
> But vacancy absorbing space,
> And fixedness—without a place;
> There were no stars—no earth—no time—
> No check—no change—no good—no crime—
> But silence, and a stirless breath
> Which neither was of life nor death;
> A sea of stagnant idleness,
> Blind, boundless, mute, and motionless!

The suggestion of similarity between the speaker's situation and the position of Coleridge's Mariner is forceful, especially in the last two lines of this passage,[4] but in this instance the situation has been rendered more complex by the fact that, thinking that he has committed no crime, the speaker cannot base his belief in an ultimately beneficent universe upon emotional acceptance of his own guilt. Hence he inhabits a world in which there appears to be no distinction between good and evil.

The speaker begins his account of regeneration in the tenth stanza. The primarily apparent quality of his ordeal appears to have been that of silence; significantly, therefore, "the carol of a bird" broke the darkness of the mind and restored "by dull degrees . . . / My senses to their wonted track." The picture that the speaker now renders, of "the glimmer of the sun / Creeping as it before had done," echoes, within a slightly altered emotional context, that in the second stanza: "A sunbeam which hath lost its way, / And through the crevice and the cleft / Of the thick wall is fallen and left." Since, for emotional survival in his universe of solitude, the speaker must become a providentialist, the bird was for him one of good omen: "A lovely bird, with azure wings, / And song that said a thousand things, / And seemed to say them all for me!" He regarded the bird empathically ("It seemed like me to want a mate") and was thereby, moving emotionally outward from the Self, brought "back to feel and think." Appropriately, then, he passed to the suggestion that (within the larger providential scheme with the center of which the speaker now clearly identifies himself) the bird might be anthropomorphic. "I know not," he remarks,

> if it were, in wingéd guise,
> A visitant from Paradise;
> For—Heaven forgive that thought! the while

> Which made me both to weep and smile—
> I sometimes deemed that it might be
> My brother's soul come down to me.

After the flight of the bird, when the speaker abandoned this suggestion, somewhat illogically and even ambiguously perhaps ("And then 'twas mortal well I knew, / For he would never thus have flown— / And left me twice to doubly lone"), he was not forsaking his belief in Providence but merely in the likelihood that the bird was a permanent agent.

"A kind of change came in my fate," the speaker recalls at the beginning of the eleventh stanza:

> My keepers grew compassionate;
> I know not what had made them so,
> They were inured to sights of woe,
> But so it was.

Though the speaker assigns no cause to the keepers' apparent change, pointedly disclaiming in fact knowledge of any, he at least implies (by his conscious use of the word "fate," his insistence that the keepers were oblivious to his "woe," and his describing their change immediately after he has told of his sympathy with the bird) that the keepers were also instruments serving the end of his growth-through-pain in an essentially just universe. But outside the speaker's own evaluation there is ample evidence that, moving from despair toward affirmation and creating a new emotional reality where for a while none had existed, only the speaker himself changed them from the cruel and impersonal "they" of the seventh stanza to "My keepers" here.

In the twelfth stanza the speaker recounts how he passed into the stage of positive affirmation. In itself this is momentous, for in his choice he had been physically restricted whether to seek death or endure life. Given freedom to walk about his cell and to make the footing by which to mount to the window, he had no desire to escape, since "the whole earth would henceforth be / A wider prison unto me," but only "to bend / Once more, upon the mountains high, / The quiet of a loving eye." As he reconstructs his experience, not Man but Nature (which he had previously regarded in large part as an abstraction, the stuff for rhetorical figures, and at best the filter for human love) became for him the object of direct affirmation, of his revived sympathies now extended beyond the bird. The distant isle stimulated once more his love of freedom, he recalls in the following stanza, but freedom expressed by Man's relation to Nature. The water itself became a full symbol of life. "The fish swam by the castle wall," he recalls, projecting his own dynamic reaffirmation, "And they seem joyous each and all." The eagle echoes the bird of the first stage of resurrection (but he is larger), again serving providentially: "Methought he never flew so fast / As then to me he seemed to fly." But soon the speaker felt frustration, suggesting perhaps that pain is a necessary condition of desire and fulfillment. What he recalls is a simple psychological reaction, exhaustion following emotional intensity and depression coming in the wake of exhaustion:

> And I felt troubled—and would fain
> I had not left my recent chain;
> And when I did descend again,
> The darkness of my dim abode
> Fell on me as a heavy load;
> It was as is a new-dug grave,
> Closing o'er one we sought to save,—
> And let my glance, too much opprest,
> Had almost need of such a rest.

Rationalized by the speaker, his depression could be derived from his philosophic awareness of his inability to attain full consummation in his love for Nature's elements. The experience is reminiscent of his reaction to the bird, but with the difference that he had now ceased to be passive, and what depression came to him resulted from the fact that he was active to the limit of his capacities.

The speaker attempts, in the concluding stanza, to give to the episode he has recounted a significance which sustains his life wish. Time has passed, but of time he has no real sense because it derives its dimensions only from space and motion, and in his affirmation the speaker has achieved only a sense of Being. "At last men came to set me free," he remarks, but what they offered was now meaningless: "I [had] learned to love despair." Consciously he believes that he is triumphant, that he has passed beyond dependence on physical surroundings; in reality he has compressed physical surroundings to the dimensions of the Self. Hence, when he remarks,

> And thus when they appeared at last,
> And all my bonds aside were cast,
> These heavy walls to me had grown
> A hermitage—and all my own!
> And half I felt as they were come
> To tear me from a second home,

though he may intend to make an assertion that is ultimately providential, he is really making a solipsistic one. In his "friendship" with the spiders which he then describes, he carried his affirmation for Nature to consistent fulfillment, drawing from it, he would seem to suggest, its full inner value for the Self. He thus achieved a sympathy that is both cosmic and (because the spiders and mice are lesser creatures than eagles or small birds) final:

> We were all inmates of one place,
> And I, the monarch of each race,

> Had power to kill—yet, strange to tell!
> In quiet we had learned to dwell;
> My very chains and I grew friends,
> So much a long communion tends
> To make us what we are:—even I
> Regained my freedom with a sigh.

The messianic impulse is obvious in his statement of the proposition of fulfillment of Self through Sorrow, toward the clear enunciation of which he has been working throughout his tale. Merely to have experienced and to understand are for the speaker emotionally insufficient: he must reconstruct and tell.

V

Manfred

Manfred IS NOT, AS IT HAS OFTEN BEEN CONSIDERED, A PLAY
that is essentially concerned with the relation between good
and evil. The frame of the morality play is in itself mislead-
ing if we fail to realize that the play deals not with external
verities that seem to strive for Manfred's spirit but with the
reaction of his spirit itself to those apparent verities: they do
not alter him, but rather in his own consciousness he creates
and destroys them, or simply fails to do so.[1] Many have
recognized the fact that *Manfred* is a one-character drama,
but few seem to have become fully aware of the implications
therein. In the several scenes in which Manfred is not actually
present, the image of his being dominates all other characters;
only as psychological subordinates do these characters themselves achieve structural significance. The question of their
origin, in other words, is not crucial and perhaps hardly
meaningful—whether they are, within the play as an extended monologue, entirely figmental, or (the earthly beings
at least) in part objectively real. Only in the impact upon the
mind of Manfred of the forces or values which these characters represent are they significant. The play is certainly not
about things; but only slightly more is it about ideas. Essentially concerned with the consciousness or the Self, it is,
broadly, a psychological rather than a philosophic drama.

In the opening, significantly in Manfred's first soliloquy,
the protagonist remarks:

97

in my heart
There is a vigil, and these eyes but close
To look within; and yet I live, and bear
The aspect and the form of breathing men.
But Grief should be the Instructor of the wise;
Sorrow is Knowledge: they who know the most
Must mourn the deepest o'er the fatal truth,
The Tree of Knowledge is not that of Life
(I, i, 5-12)

Manfred approaches a phase possibly described as total intellectual awareness, but this does not involve emotional
response. Failing to bring affirmation, Knowledge seems necessarily then to bring Sorrow. Though the substance for the
synthesis which he seeks to achieve in his being remains intellectual, the force which would inform it is necessarily emotional. The protagonist has attempted to bring Truth ("Philosophy and science, and the springs / Of Wonder, and the
wisdom of the World") within the structure of the consciousness and to direct Goodness toward other men, but
these have remained essentially apart from the Self: "Good—
or evil—life— / Powers, passions—all I see in other beings, /
Have been to me as rain unto the sands." Since the moment of
Manfred's Fall, from which dates all emotional failure, is
simply "that all-nameless hour," the cause is necessarily also
unnamed; though a sin or crime, it presumably bears, ironically though consistently, no emotional impact. "I have no
dread," Manfred remarks, concluding this phase of his soliloquy, "And feel the curse to have no natural fear, / Nor
fluttering throb, that beats with hopes or wishes, / Or lurking
love of something on the earth."

The Spirits whom Manfred invokes assume choral parts,
individually and then collectively. Each of the first six asks
him his wish; the seventh scorns him, but in so doing com-

ments upon the nature of his essential problem. The Spirit of the Star ruling Manfred's destiny, it recounts how the Star itself, once upon a course "free and regular," became, at the arrival of "the Hour" (of the Fall of Man? the time of the coming to Man of an insatiable desire for knowledge?), "A pathless Comet, and a curse, / The menace of the Universe." Manfred, born thereafter beneath its influence, would necessarily become a mixture of qualities of (intellectual?) greatness and (emotional?) failure:

> Thou worm! whom I obey and scorn—
> Forced by a Power (which is not thine,
> And lent thee but to make thee mine)
> For this brief moment to descend,
> Where these weak Spirits round thee bend
> And parley with a thing like thee—
> What would'st thou, Child of Clay! with me?
> (I, i, 110-31)

The essence of Manfred's desire is "Oblivion—self-oblivion," rather than annihilation, the power to deny feeling rather than to cease to feel and move. The Spirits are unable to give this, most obviously because they themselves are aspects of Mind whereas Manfred's problem remains of course emotional: put simply, affirmation cannot be externally induced. Only the figure of the woman in which the Seventh Spirit momentarily appears, presumably in the image of one we come to recognize as Astarte, moves Manfred. The Incantation following her disappearance contains what is fundamentally a description of Manfred's psychological state, an emotional incapacity to desire either to live or to die.

Like the first scene, the second opens with Manfred's soliloquy, in which in this instance he emphasizes the solitude of his position and rejects dependence "on superhuman aid," which has "no power upon the past, and for / The future,

till the past be gulfed in darkness, / It is not of my search."
Manfred's problem, which must be solved (if at all) by emotional rather than intellectual means, is to achieve a unity in
Time of the phases of the Self, principally those before and
after his Fall, and in so doing establish a basis for a relationship between the Self and all outside of it. That he fails
largely accounts for what is to be the conclusion of his
struggle, by which, neither victor nor vanquished, he remains
in juxtaposition to all that surrounds him at the moment of
death. Manfred continues his soliloquy, understanding perfectly the essence of his problem, positive and negative emotional incapacity, toward which he can of course have no
reaction. Implicitly recalling his earlier remarks concerning
his failure to yoke Truth and Goodness within his consciousness, he now laments:

> My Mother Earth!
> And thou fresh-breaking Day, and you, ye Mountains,
> Why are ye beautiful? I cannot love ye.
> And thou, the bright Eye of the Universe,
> That openest over all, and unto all
> Art a delight—thou shin'st not in my heart
>
> (I, ii, 7-12)

Nor do the "crags, upon whose extreme edge / I stand," the
symbolic antithesis to the sun, suggest suicide with a force
sufficient to overcome the

> power upon me which withholds,
> And makes it my fatality to live,—
> If it be life to wear within myself
> This barrenness of Spirit, and to be
> My own Soul's sepulchre, for I have ceased
> To justify my deeds unto myself—
> The last infirmity of evil.

He has become Self without motive, presumably the inevitable conclusion of intellectual Man, who by his very nature is isolated from all about him and in whose being itself the unity of his intellectual Truth with moving Beauty and Goodness is beyond possibility:

> Beautiful!
> How beautiful is all this visible world!
> How glorious in its action and itself!
> But we, who name ourselves its sovereigns, we,
> Half dust, half deity, alike unfit
> To sink or soar, with our mixed essences make
> A conflict of its elements, and breathe
> The breath of degradation and of pride,
> Contending with low wants and lofty will,
> Till our Mortality predominates,
> And men are—what they name not to themselves,
> And trust not to each other.

Manfred hears the shepherd's pipe, and the Chamois Hunter soon enters. The situation is ironic, for both have come to the precipice on a quest, though of very different kinds. The Hunter at once perceives Manfred's danger, not from himself but from the elements about him; Manfred slowly perceives that perhaps through Nature's act, essentially external to him, will he achieve (though not "Oblivion—self-oblivion") annihilation by death. Their somewhat parallel speeches are illustrative:

> *C. Hun.* The mists begin to rise from up the valley;
> I'll warn him to descend, or he may chance
> To lose at once his way and life together.

> *Man.* The mist boil up around the glaciers; clouds
> Rise curling fast beneath me, white and sulphury,
> Like foam from the roused ocean of deep Hell,

> Whose every wave breaks on a living shore,
> Heaped with the damned like pebbles.—I am giddy.

Only as the Chamois Hunter comes forth to save Manfred from apparent accident does Manfred seemingly move toward suicide. The Hunter's behavior is clearly the norm, neither grand nor low, and Manfred's, in its extremes, the abnormal. That Manfred is apparently able, for this brief moment, to make a clear denial of life, which he has been unable to do before and cannot do again, seems totally inconsistent with what has been revealed of the nature of Manfred's problem. The difficulty is resolved only if we regard the scene as a projection of Manfred's inner struggle, in which he himself enacts the death impulse (more familiarly put, perhaps, a motivation of the id) and the Chamois Hunter the restraining force (the superego).

The Chamois Hunter opens the second act with an assertion to Manfred, the real meaning of which the Hunter himself could not comprehend: "thou must not yet go forth: / Thy mind and body are alike unfit / To trust each other." To this he adds a qualification in which he unknowingly foretells Manfred's death: "for some hours at least." As Manfred himself has already recognized, his psychological situation arises essentially from his dualistic nature as Man, which, moreover, is reflected in the universe that he sees, constructed upon antitheses of light and dark, good and evil, action and inaction. Manfred's reply, at one level trivial, is revealing: "I do know / My route full well, and need no further guidance." Here he anticipates his subsequent rejection of both the Abbot and the Demons, though his explicit reference is obviously intellectual rather than emotional. Significantly it is the Hunter, already established as representing the norm of human behavior, who draws from Manfred an explicit description of his "sin":

I say 'tis blood—my blood! the pure warm stream
Which ran in the veins of my fathers, and in ours
When we were in our youth, and had one heart,
And loved each other as we should not love,
And this was shed.

But, again characteristically, the Hunter fails to comprehend the meaning of Manfred's words and urges "patience" as a means of assuaging what he believes to be the pain of guilt, but Manfred necessarily rejects this, emphasizing in another way the nature of his essential problem. The word "patience" is "For brutes of burthen, not for birds of prey!" he says. "Preach it to mortals of a dust like thine,— / I am not of thine order." In reply to the Hunter's comment upon Manfred's apparent agedness, Manfred touches upon the other aspect of his situation, the relation of the Self to Time, concluding with an assertion of the mechanical nature of any seeming continuity of the phases of the consciousness:

Think'st thou existence doth depend on time?
It doth; but actions are our epochs: mine
Have made my days and nights imperishable,
Endless, and all alike, as sands on the shore,
Innumerable atoms.

The Hunter, necessarily making a personal comparison, proposes that Manfred is mad, to which Manfred replies: "I would I were—for then the things I see / Would be but a distempered dream." Paradoxically, in Manfred's solipsistic universe, his own madness must be inconceivable. The scene concludes as Manfred rejects all aid—that of the weaker man (which would be useless to him) or that sought by prayers to Heaven (which would demand from Manfred the affirmation that, by the very nature of his affliction, he could not give).

In the second scene Manfred is alone in an Alpine Valley.

"No eyes / But mine now drink this sight of loveliness; / I should be sole in this sweet solitude," he says, "And with the Spirit of the place divide / The homage of these waters." (II, ii, 8-12). He summons the Witch of the Alps, to him the "Beautiful Spirit," representing one of the transcendental forces (like the Truth and Goodness to which he has already openly referred) which he would have the Self assimilate. Asked by the Spirit what he will have, Manfred replies, merely

> To look upon thy beauty—nothing further.
> The face of the earth hath maddened me, and I
> Take refuge in her mysteries, and pierce
> To the abodes of those who govern her—
> But they can nothing aid me. I have sought
> From them what they could not bestow, and now
> I search no further.

Asked again of his will, Manfred traces his isolation ("From my youth upwards / My Spirit walked not with the souls of men, / Nor looked upon the earth with human eyes"), to which there was the single exception, "One who—but of her anon." He first attempted to find total emotional fulfillment in Nature, but, unable to escape his own humanity, he failed: "I felt myself degraded back to them [men], / And was all clay again." He then sought resolution of his own problem through learning, but the intellectual means was inconsistent with his end and seemed to lead to his Fall. It is significant that the form taken by the Fall was incest, since explicitly Astarte herself is an image of Manfred's being. "She was like me in lineaments," he remarks, in all ways except his faults. "Her virtues were her own." Consistently, therefore, he "loved her, and destroyed her!" He himself has come to "dwell in my despair" (a state which theologically may involve the ultimate sin but in the present instance can be taken only as that which is clearly beyond either positive or negative emotional affirmation), from which he would have the Spirit of Beauty remove him. She offers aid, to be given "if thou / Wilt swear obedience to my will, and do / My bidding." As in all other instances, however, could he emotionally give her the assurance requested, he would not need her aid. He dismisses the Witch.

Manfred now intends what is antithetical to his positive quest for the fusion and assimilation of transcendental values:

> I have one resource
> Still in my science—I can call the dead,
> And ask them what it is we dread to be:
> The sternest answer can but be the Grave,
> And that is nothing.

His present position is, as he realizes in part, paradoxical, a reflection of his total situation: "If I had never lived, that which I love / Had still been living; had I never loved, / That which I love would still be beautiful." Had he never willed and sought, he would not now be emotionally inactive. He now "dread[s] the thing I dare," hesitating "to gaze / On spirit, good or evil" and "feel[ing] a strange cold thaw upon my heart."

Containing the short choral speeches of the Destinies and the Voices, the third scene of the second act can be regarded as simply a projection, introduced by Manfred's closing words in the second scene, "The Night approaches." It leads to the scene in the Hall of Arimanes, one who is clearly the antithesis to the Witch of the Alps (the Spirit of Beauty) and a foil to Manfred himself. Ordered to kneel before Arimanes, Manfred refuses. Having "sunk before my vain despair, and knelt / To my own desolation," Manfred remarks, he can give emotional acceptance to none else, either to the projected image of the Negative and Evil or (as he has demonstrated) to that of Beauty. "Bid *him* bow down to that which is above him," Manfred says of Arimanes, "The overruling Infinite— the Maker / Who made him not for worship—let him kneel, / And we will kneel together." Only if Evil acknowledges Good can Manfred accept the reality of the power of Arimanes; but this cannot be, for Arimanes represents one side of Manfred's intellectual view of the cosmic antithesis, which, however, remains for Manfred emotionally unreal (he is aware of the fact of his Fall but cannot actively feel guilt for it), or he would not now be among the Spirits in the Hall of Arimanes.

By what the First Destiny now describes as "his knowledge, and his powers and will, / As far as is compatible with clay," Manfred has evoked these and other Spirits; though he has not reached the point at which they become for him emotional realities, he still rejects the proposition that he must ultimately fail in his attempts to revive the emotional forces that once were his. According to Manfred's wish and with Arimanes' permission (as a projection he could give no other), Nemesis calls forth the Spirit of Astarte. She seems substantial in the same way that Manfred's own acts have given the first appearance of deriving from real motivation. "But now I see it is no living hue, / But a strange hectic," he then realizes, "like the unnatural red / Which Autumn plants upon the perished leaf." Astarte is here essentially as she has been described in the earliest scenes, an image of Manfred himself. Asked now to confirm or deny the emotional reality of his guilt ("No, / I cannot speak to her—but bid her speak— / Forgive me or condemn me"), she does neither. The death of Manfred which she foretells is rendered inevitable: by his failure to achieve either forgiveness or condemnation he now demonstrates what he has to this point rejected, that his attempts to move from the position of emotional inaction are

necessarily without expectation. In the conclusion of the first
act Manfred attempted death, but at the conclusion of the
second act, when death is foretold, he is fully aware that in
itself death will offer no solace. "She's gone, and will not be
recalled," he remarks after the disappearance of the Spirit of
Astarte. "Her words will be fulfilled. Return to the earth."
Manfred has reached absolute despair.

In the first scene of the third act, the Abbot of St. Maurice,
approaching Manfred (who feels "a calm . . . / [an] Inexplicable stillness! which till now / Did not belong to what I
knew of life"), reveals that he has heard "thou holdest converse with the things / Which are forbidden to the search of
man." The Abbot, however, cannot recognize the fact that the
nature of such "converse" intellectually and (of greater significance) emotionally prevents his touching Manfred. The
Abbot points to Divine retribution, but fear of this, which
must rest upon the desire to perpetuate the Self, is for Manfred clearly meaningless. The exchange between them becomes tedious, but this fact simply emphasizes the remoteness
of Manfred from the Abbot and his image of an organized
universe. The scene itself, following Manfred's vision of
Astarte, dramatizes the totality of emotional inaction to which
Manfred has been led by that vision. The Abbot, like the
Chamois Hunter, is a human agent apparently working
toward the redemption of Manfred; but between their appearances Manfred has had "converse" with both the Spirit
of Beauty and Arimanes, concluding his search and reaching
his emotional climax with the vision of Astarte, so that though
the Hunter encountered one still able to seek fulfillment in
death, the Abbot tries to move one who has passed to ultimate
despair. The fact that the latter is a religious simply intensifies the difference in the kinds of failure regarding Manfred
which they represent. Thus, the third act does not appear to
reveal a spiritual elevation from the level of the action of the

second, as has been suggested;[2] rather, it depicts the necessary progression from Manfred's emotional climax in the second act.

The next scene and much of the third, containing Manfred's farewell apostrophe to the sun (which has been for him a symbol of the positive desire for life) and the dialogue between Herman and Manual, have but limited dramatic function. The Abbot then approaches and wishes to see Manfred once more, thereby following the intention which he stated at the close of the first scene and moving toward what is to be his dramatic function at the time of Manfred's death. In the fourth scene, Manfred, alone in his tower, recalls his youthful love of beauty, lost upon his intellectual quest:

> 'Twas such a night!
> 'Tis strange that I recall it at this time;
> But I have found our thoughts take wildest flight
> Even at the moment when they should array
> Themselves in pensive order.

But "pensive order" also has long ceased to promise reality. The Abbot enters and unknowingly describes Manfred's essential position:

> My good Lord!
> I crave a second grace for this approach;
> But yet let not my humble zeal offend
> By its abruptness—all it hath of ill
> Recoils on me; its good in the effect
> May light upon your head—could I say *heart*—
> Could I touch *that,* with words or prayers, I should
> Recall a noble spirit which hath wandered,
> But is not yet all lost.

In his final assertion the Abbot assumes an emotional potential where there is none. Though, like Manfred, the Abbot seems unafraid of the Spirits which soon appear, his hope is qualified by them. The Abbot holds the orthodox concept of evil as privation of good: "Avaunt! ye evil ones!—Avaunt! I say,— / Ye have no power where Piety hath power, / And I do charge ye in the name—." To Manfred the Spirits are equally unreal, but only because of his total emotional isolation from all good and evil: "Away! I'll die as I have lived— alone." The leading Spirit insists upon Manfred's obligation, incurred through Manfred's sorcery. But his plight is that of the intellectual rather than of the magician, Manfred asserts:

> Thou false fiend, thou liest!
> My life is in its last hour,—*that* I know,
> Nor would redeem a moment of that hour;
> I do not combat against Death, but thee
> And thy surrounding angels; my past power
> Was purchased by no compact with thy crew,
> But by superior science—penance, daring,
> And length of watching, strength of mind, and skill
> In knowledge of our Fathers—when the earth
> Saw men and spirits walking side by side,
> And gave ye no supremacy: I stand
> Upon my strength—I do defy—deny—
> Spurn back, and scorn ye!—

Despite the intellectual denial of the reality of evil, which the Abbot has just made explicit, he *feels* that evil is a necessary antithesis to good; he cannot, therefore, comprehend Manfred's situation. Manfred neither conceives of nor feels the reality of good *or* evil; only the final and total isolation of the Self, which (psychologically as well as philosophically) renders death necessary, constitutes reality. Resignation, achieved through emotional incapacity and then total despair, has thus become ironically the only positive value for the Self:

Back to thy hell!
Thou hast no power upon me, *that* I feel;
Thou never shalt possess me, *that* I know:
What I have done is done; I bear within
A torture which could nothing gain from thine:
The mind which is immortal makes itself
Requital for its good or evil thoughts,—
Is its own origin of ill and end—
And its own place and time: its innate sense,
When stripped of this mortality, derives
No colour from the fleeting things without,
But is absorbed in sufferance or in joy,
Born from the knowledge of its own desert.
Thou didst not tempt me, and thou couldst not tempt me;
I have not been thy dupe, nor am thy prey—
But was my own destroyer, and will be
My own hereafter.—Back, ye baffled fiends!
The hand of Death is on me—but not yours!

The Demons disappear. Manfred ignores the Abbot's final request that he pray, thereby rejecting the agency of the other side of the supposed universal moral dichotomy. The effects of physical decay outwardly resemble the emotional results of Manfred's intellectual quest. "My dull eyes can fix thee not," he remarks to the Abbot. "But all things swim around me, and the earth / Heaves as it were beneath me." In the total acceptance that brings its own solace ("Old man! 'tis not so difficult to die"), Manfred expires, leaving the Abbot to conjecture upon, but not to understand, the nature of his death.

VI

The Lament of Tasso,
Mazeppa, and
The Prophecy of Dante

i

CRITICISM OF *The Lament of Tasso* HAS BEEN CONCERNED PRIN-
cipally with the historical accuracy of Byron's picture of
Tasso rather than with the structure of that picture. This
approach has been reasonable to the extent that the poet poses
the question of accuracy by choosing a figure from literary history about whom a group of associations clusters; but those
taking this approach have not achieved their desired ends,
partly because in ignoring the structure of the picture, they
have necessarily failed to judge its accuracy. Since *The
Lament of Tasso* is a monologue, our first endeavor in reading
the poem should be to comprehend the substance of what
Tasso reveals, at both the intentional and the unconscious
levels. Thereafter we can make meaningful judgments, historical and aesthetic, of the poem's achievement.

The pivotal concern of *The Lament of Tasso* is madness,
arising quite expectedly from the fact of the speaker's confinement. That Tasso denies outright madness in the opening
of the poem but comes to admit a degree of disturbance
somewhat later is quite apparent.[1] Of greater significance is

the manner in which he demonstrates the nature of his mental state. In the opening lines of the poem he is obviously reversing what to his captors is the normal course of affairs, for he sees himself as one who is not confined because he is mad but, instead, is afflicted with a canker of the mind because he has been confined:

> Long years!—It tries the thrilling frame to bear
> And eagle-spirit of a Child of Song—
> Long years of outrage—calumny—and wrong;
> Imputed madness, prisoned solitude,
> And the Mind's canker in its savage mood,
> When the impatient thirst of light and air
> Parches the heart; and the abhorred grate,
> Marring the sunbeams with its hideous shade,
> Works through the throbbing eyeball to the brain,
> With a hot sense of heaviness and pain
>
> 1-10)

The heart itself, affected as much as the brain, images for him both poetic inspiration and the impulse which is at once the cause for his confinement and the means by which he will justify his being and actions in a hostile world. The justification itself, however, is somewhat less than rationally ordered. After briefly describing the conditions "in the cave / Which is my lair, and—it may be—my grave," Tasso remarks, with perhaps surprising moderation: "All this hath somewhat worn me, and may wear, / But must be borne. I stoop not to despair." He immediately associates his present resoluteness with the *Gerusalemme:*

> For I have battled with mine agony,
> And made me wings wherewith to overfly
> The narrow circus of my dungeon wall,
> And freed the Holy Sepulchre from thrall;
> And revelled among men and things divine,

And poured my spirit over Palestine,
In honour of the sacred war for Him,
The God who was on earth and is in Heaven,
For He has strengthened me in heart and limb.
That through this sufferance I might be forgiven,
I have employed my penance to record
How Salem's shrine was won, and how adored.

The process of literary creation which he describes seems to be in the present, so that surprise follows the speaker's sudden revelation: "But this is o'er—my pleasant task is done:— / My long-sustaining Friend of many years!" He rapidly intensifies his expression (the "Friend" easily becomes "my Soul's child") and falls into a mixed but revealing metaphor: the "child[,] / Which ever playing round me came and smiled, / And wooed me from myself with thy sweet sight." He soon makes the faltering admission: "Thou too art ended —what is left me now? / For I have anguish yet to bear—and how?" The answer *implied* in the question itself obviously conflicts with the earlier assertion ("I stoop not to despair") and the explicit response which follows the question: "I know not that—but in the innate force / Of my own spirit shall be found resource."

Quite simply, there are in Tasso's consciousness two images of the Self, one of a being indomitable and the other of "a broken reed" with its "last bruise," and much of the tension in the poem arises from the conflict between them. As this becomes crucial and appears to be unresolvable, the speaker seems to break away from what has led to an awareness of the conflict and, as it were, begins again. Thus he quickly protests his guiltlessness in the present confinement as well as his sanity, and turns to what he believes is the real cause for his incarceration and a basis for his maintaining the image of the indomitable Self:

> I have not sunk, for I had no remorse,
> Nor cause for such: they called me mad—and why?
> Oh Leonora! wilt not *thou* reply?
> I was indeed delirious in my heart
> To lift my love so lofty as thou art;
> But still my frenzy was not of the mind:
> I knew my fault, and feel my punishment
> Not less because I suffer it unbent.

The thematic distinction between mind and heart is essential to his recurring protest of innocence and sanity, for he has willed no evil: "That thou wert beautiful, and I not blind, / Hath been the sin which shuts me from mankind." He has reached the point of making a substitution for the emotional sustenance given him by the composition of the *Gerusalemme;* it is worth observing that in his rationale the love for Leonora, which we might expect to be his primary mover, now at least appears to become the substitute for literary composition as the source of psychological endurance:

> But let them [mankind] go, or torture as they will,
> My heart can multiply thine image still;
> Successful Love may sate itself away;
> The wretchéd are the faithful; 'tis their fate
> To have all feeling, save the one, decay,
> And every passion into one dilate,
> As rapid rivers into Ocean pour;
> But ours is fathomless, and hath no shore.

His assertion is fully messianic. With all the satisfaction that self-sacrifice brings comes a fusion, for the moment at least, of the two images of the Self, one of the "wretchéd" and the other of the "faithful"; the word "decay" foretells a later occurrence, when he is nearly to admit the full psychological implications of such wretchedness.

The theme of isolation dominates the third stanza. Conditioned by "the long and maniac cry / Of minds and bodies in captivity" and by his keepers ("Some who do still goad on the o'er-laboured mind, / And dim the little light that's left behind / With needless torture"), Tasso emotionally rejects both: "With these and with their victims am I classed." He first finds hope only in ultimate isolation, death itself, but in the beginning of the fourth stanza the image of the "broken reed" has yielded for the moment to that of the indomitable Self: "I have been patient, let me be so yet; / I had forgotten half I would forget, / But it revives." Memory, oppressing the weaker Self, aids the stronger, fixing for him an image of the injustice which he must endure. The word "half" is crucial, for what he remembers of "this vast Lazar-house of many woes" is the substance of an image of a half-world, a fragmentary universe:

> Where laughter is not mirth, nor thought the mind,
> Nor words a language, nor ev'n men mankind;
> Where cries reply to curses, shrieks to blows,
> And each is tortured in his separate hell—
> For we are crowded in our solitudes—
> Many, but each divided by the wall,
> Which echoes Madness in her babbling moods;
> While all can hear, none heed his neighbor's call.

The image is subjectively directed: the fact that the speaker views his surroundings but cannot relate the elements of what he views except in terms of his divided image of the Self is obvious evidence of his own "separate hell"; yet at the point at which he nearly accepts the suggestion of his own madness, he withdraws: "None [heeds his neighbor's call]! save that One, the veriest wretch of all, / Who was not made to be the mate of these, / Nor bound between Distraction and Disease." His messianic satisfactions are fully apparent. He now returns to the question, from which the last eleven lines (84-94) constitute a digression: "Feel I not wroth with those who placed me here? / Who have debased me in the minds of men, / Debarring me the usage of my own [?]" The answer, implied perhaps in the question, is made explicit: "No!— still too proud to be vindictive—I / Have pardoned Princes' insults, and would die." His love for Leonora, he protests, precludes the possibility of hatred. The stanza closes.

Insisting that his "love . . . knows not to despair, / But all unquenched is still my better part," Tasso now apostrophizes Leonora: his love, "Dwelling deep in my shut and silent heart" (like "the gathered lightning in its cloud, / Encompassed with its dark and rolling shroud, / Till struck"), flashed suddenly forth "through my frame" at the mention of her name, bringing the recollected image of her and "all things as they were." The figure is mixed with the word "shroud," which faintly suggests a relation between his love and death. After the passing of the recollected image, he is as he was, imprisoned and restrained, essentially unaffected: "I am the same." He moves directly toward a deification of Leonora, which is quite consistent with his function as poet, based first upon her appearance (Love "arrayed / Thy lineaments in beauty that dismayed— / Oh! not dismayed—but awed, like One above!"), then upon a causative relationship: "I know not how—thy Genius mastered mine— / My Star stood still before thee."

It is significant that in the fifth stanza the speaker has insisted that his love "was / Sufficient to itself, its own reward," that he has loved "without design." He has been put to some pains to develop a seemingly rational structure to explain how, in his present confinement, his love knowing no despair has become a substitute for the composition of the *Gerusalemme*. In his explanation he has, it would seem, reversed the usual roles of human love and sublimational action. We approach the point underlying the irony in the poem and much of its development hereafter: Tasso's love for Leonora is unconsciously significant because, from any viewpoint he might assume, it is primarily a tribute to him rather than to her. The fact (with which he concludes the sixth stanza) that "*Thou* didst annihilate the earth to me!" is derivative not from her power to attract but from his power to love, with which in the sixth stanza itself the speaker is most concerned.

"It is no marvel," he begins, that he can endure the pains which he has experienced for his love of Leonora: "from my very birth / My soul was drunk with Love,—which did pervade / And mingle with whate'er I saw on earth." And each experience, creating from the flowers and rocks a Paradise of love ("Where I did lay me down within the shade / Of waving trees, and dreamed uncounted hours"), was proleptic of this present. Even the reactions to what he did and the persecution that he suffered foretold (or so to him it now seems) his imprisonment for love; "the Wise," shaking "their white agéd heads o'er me," declared, with unknowing prophecy, "Of such materials wretched men were made, / And such a truant boy would end in woe, / And that the only lesson was a blow." Beaten by them, "I did not weep, / But cursed them in my heart, and to my haunt / Returned and wept alone." But in the present there is no anger, since "with my years my soul began to pant / With feelings of strange tumult and soft pain; / And the whole heart exhaled into One Want," which remained undefined until he found Leonora: "And then I lost my being, all to be / Absorbed in thine." Although *in recollection* the discovery of Leonora offered him the opportunity for fulfillment that nothing else would, his emphasis throughout the stanza has been upon himself, who in his own mind assumes the capacity for self-annihilating love.

In the seventh stanza the speaker is concerned with two instances of irony, of which he himself is aware of only the

first. "I loved all Solitude," he recollects, but he had not expected to pass what remains of life "remote / From all com-
munion with existence, save / The maniac and his tyrant." [2]
But by its very nature the second example of irony must be
hidden from the speaker: Tasso himself has gradually approached what he protests he is not. "Had I been / Their
fellow, many years ere this had seen / My mind like theirs
corrupted to its grave," he remarks. "But who hath seen me
writhe, or heard me rave?" Only to the outsider can the contradiction become apparent. In the force that he brings to his
protests, Tasso makes it clear that, at an unconscious level,
they are, if anything, compensatory. The stanza closes as the
speaker compares himself to "the wrecked sailor on his desert
shore," whose "world is all before him," so that "though *he*
perish, he may lift his eye, / And with a dying glance upbraid the sky"; the speaker's world "is *here,* / Scarce twice
the space they must accord my bier," so that, as he insists with
supreme unawareness of the irony that he reveals, "I will not
raise my own [glance] in such reproof, / Although 'tis clouded
by my dungeon roof."

Yet Tasso soon admits to some degree what he has long
been denying: "I feel at times my mind decline, / But with
a sense of its decay." Unlike those around him, with whom he
has consistently contrasted himself, he is aware of what is
happening, he insists with unconscious irony: he sees "a
strange Demon, who is vexing me / With pilfering pranks and
petty pains, below / The feeling of the healthful and the
free." To the substance of the hallucination the speaker
attributes spiritual reality, suggesting that the Demon may be
an agent of "Powers of Evil" that fill the vacuum created
because "Heaven forgets me." He thus actualized the full
potential of the image of the "broken reed" Self ("One, who
long hath suffered so, / Sickness of heart, and narrowness of

place, / And all that may be borne, or can debase"), against which the image of the heroic Self stands intact: "in this furnace" his spirit, "like steel in tempering fire," has been proved, "Because I loved what not to love, and see, / Was more or less than mortal, and than me." If Tasso were really to regard the world in a verifiable perspective such as sane men presumably hold, he would see the Demon as hallucinational and would not involve it in his less than rational attempt to synthesize the two images of the Self; but then, clearly as sane as he protests he is, he would of course not see the Demon at all.

The concluding stanza begins with Tasso's assertion of his present imperviousness to the pains of prison ("My scars are callous, or I should have dashed / My brain against these bars, as the sun flashed / In mockery through them"), recalling the description in the opening lines of "the abhorred grate" working "through the throbbing eyeball to the brain." Then he was simply protesting his sanity; he has now worked to a position somewhat more complex; despite his many promises never to upbraid, to hate, or to surrender, the speaker has, to some extent, done all, and here he insists that he will not commit suicide. First, of course, he has become hardened, he suggests; actually the heroic Self always triumphs at the final moment so that the "broken reed" Self will not destroy both. Secondly, since suicide would substantiate the charge of madness, the failure to commit suicide would, Tasso perhaps implies, exonerate him:

> 'tis that I would not die
> And sanction with self-slaughter the dull lie
> Which snared me here, and with the brand of shame
> Stamp Madness deep into my memory,
> And woo Compassion to a blighted name,
> Sealing the sentence which my foes proclaim.

The final suggestion is somewhat ambiguous, for the sentence imposed upon him has been of course to a madhouse, reasons for which suicide would substantiate; but for a suicide the sentence would also be to hell, which for Tasso the madhouse clearly resembles.

There is, however, a third reason that he refrains from self-destruction, one which externally remains an aspect of a poetic convention but in this instance has messianic implications as well: Tasso refuses what would be a release from pain so that through his art his cause may somehow triumph. His name "shall be immortal," and he will "make / A future temple of my present cell, / Which nations yet shall visit for my sake." Ferrara shall be remembered for "A Poet's wreath" and not the ducal crown. But, above all, this image of the future contains a prophecy of the union of Tasso's name with Leonora's, in which the speaker quite expectedly finds the ultimate fulfillment of both images that he holds of the Self:

> But *Thou*—when all that Birth and Beauty throws
> Of magic round thee is extinct—shalt have
> One half the laurel which o'ershades my grave.
> No power in death can tear our names apart,
> As none in life could rend thee from my heart.
> Yes, Leonora! it shall be our fate
> To be entwined for ever—but too late!

ii

Mazeppa is at once both more serious and more humorous than has been suggested. From the time of its publication many of those commenting upon it have taken the view that it demonstrates either a lack of creative seriousness on the part of the poet or a failure to understand his subject, for the final scene in the poem, in which Charles XII is discovered to have been sleeping for an hour when Mazeppa ends.

his story, has seemed discordant, in fact destructive of the emotional intensity which the story has developed.[3] But this view does not represent a full understanding of the relation between the situation in which Mazeppa finds himself and the tale which that situation frames, to which the emotional reaction on the part of Mazeppa himself becomes the object of a satire that implies the essential question of the poem—whether experience can yield an organized moral view of the universe such as Mazeppa has appeared to develop. The central character in the poem is a garrulous old man who recounts his youthful adventure in such a way that it becomes the basis for belief in a providential system that will render the present experience endurable. Within the context of the situation, Mazeppa's attempt at rationalization appears absurd, and the abrupt close of the poem, following the end of the story, is justified.

In the opening, the narrator, describing the situation of Charles and his band, assumes a position that is clearly anti-providential, against which the tale of Mazeppa, with all of its implications, is to be set. It is because "Fortune [had] left the royal Swede" that the Russians were victorious at Pultowa, simply a matter of "the hazard of the die," by which "the wounded Charles was taught to fly"; war itself is fickle, its "power and glory" as "Faithless as their vain votaries, men." Hiding for the night with his followers, Charles himself emerges as "Kinglike," one whose confidence needs no justification: he has "made, in this extreme of ill, / His pangs the vassals of his will: / And all silent and subdued were they." Attributing his plight either to Fate or to chance, he simply accepts it for what it is. But such is not the case with Mazeppa, who must justify the hope that he would now feel, by constructing out of his recollections a story demonstrating that though men approach close to death, some are released by providential intervention from what would appear to be inevitable. Mazeppa's tale becomes for him the object of psychological necessity, though for Charles it remains what the royal Swede calls it in the beginning, an inducement to sleep.[4]

The story which Mazeppa tells is very simple. He recalls the affair which he had in his "twentieth spring" with the youthful wife of an old count, the discovery of the situation, his punishment by being strapped to a wild horse that was driven into the night, his rescue and recovery after the exhaustion and death of the horse, and finally his revenge upon those who had punished him. But in the telling Mazeppa frequently becomes digressive, revealing more about himself than he recognizes. His obvious remarks on the inarticulate signs of early love ("ten thousand tones and signs / We hear and see, but none defines") become tedious at once. And his rather lengthy explanation that "the sons of pleasure," who have "nought to hope and nought to leave," "die calm, or calmer, oft than he / Whose heritage was Misery" is disproved by his own recollections and his present desire to survive, for he regards the future in exactly the manner that he attributes to the wretch just described: "To-morrow would have given him all, / Repaid his pangs, repaired his fall." Though he admits that the Count "had good reason" for his anger, Mazeppa recalls his experience without any suggestion of repentance. Revenge, in fact, becomes the only real motive stimulated by his punishment, and in recounting the episode he breaks sequence to reveal that he has "paid their insult back again":

> They little thought that day of pain,
> When launched, as on the lightning's flash,
> They bade me to destruction dash,
> That one day I should come again,
> With twice five thousand horse, to thank
> The Count for his uncourteous ride.

In his revenge Mazeppa finds the ultimate fact of his experience, enforcing for him the meaning of his story, that "Time at last sets all things even." Were this not the case, presumably he would not then have chosen this story, which illustrates rather than reveals what is essential for him to believe as he rests in hiding with King Charles, that "Time" becomes a condition of Providence, of which he, Mazeppa, is ultimately both the instrument and the object. But time is important for him in another way, for he must make the earlier episode and the meaning which he has imposed upon it ever close to the experience of the moment. In the intensity of his recollection he moves from the past tense to the present (391-92, 695-708), and in his strong underlying desire to yoke the two experiences he makes reference to the present situation from remembrance of the past: "I watched her as a sentinel, / (May ours this dark night watch as well!)." He insists that time has not weakened him ("With years, ye know, have not declined / My strength—my courage—or my mind") and that, once saved by Providence, he is fit to be saved again: "I have bared my brow / Full in Death's face— before—and now."

The story as it is told by Mazeppa becomes, therefore, another of ordeal and survival in which the survivor seems to have been elect. The solitary nature of the experience is essential. The tale is not unlike the more traditional stories of fall and redemption, of death and rebirth, except that in the words of the garrulous and egoistic old man it becomes an unconscious travesty of these: there is sin but no atonement, rescue but no salvation, recollection but no selfless understanding. The mad ride, with its sheer horror, is like a grotesque imitation of the Night Journey: the "wild wood" itself, the troop of wolves, and the herd of wild horses become the terrors that are part of the trial, leading to the final ordeal, in which Mazeppa lies bound to the fallen horse, "The dying on the dead." Uncertainty and fear characterize his recurring approaches to death: "My heart turned sick, my brain grew sore, / And throbbed awhile, then beat no more: / The skies spun like a mighty wheel." Despite temporary revival (as in the crossing of the stream, in which, he recalls, his "stiffened limbs were rebaptized"), he is for the most part suspended in a state that seems to fall between life and death.[5] At the moment of supreme terror, with the approach of the wild horses, he is suddenly spared, abandoned "to my despair, / Linked to the dead and stiffening wretch," only to come toward death again, now with seeming finality ("A gasp—a throb—a start of pain, / A sigh—and nothing more"), which gives emphasis to the fact of his rescue. The "Cossack maid" who nurses Mazeppa back to health becomes in his mind, therefore, an agent of Providence, by which he "*was released* / From adding to the vulture's feast" (italics mine). The fact that *he* was saved and lived to achieve revenge, that "They brought me into life again— / Me—one day o'er their realm to reign," gives empirical support to the assertion:

> Let none despond, let none despair!
> To-morrow the Borysthenes
> May see our coursers graze at ease
> Upon his Turkish bank.

The final pronouncement of the old Hetman is for him the emotional climax of his story, the point at which its full meaning is brought to bear on the present situation, but for the more "Kinglike" Charles that point occurred an hour ago.

iii

The speaker in *The Prophecy of Dante,* like Tasso and Mazeppa, is one who has been placed by men and circumstances in a position from which it becomes emotionally necessary for him to demonstrate the ultimate meaningfulness of the universe by asserting the triumph of Self. His speech, somewhat prolonged, reveals both intellectual and psychological progression. Unlike the protagonists in the two poems just considered, however, Dante is frequently not unaware of the implied significance of what he says. For this reason the content of his utterance can be more readily accepted. *The Prophecy of Dante* itself may be regarded as a political poem in the way that *The Prisoner of Chillon* and *The Lament of Tasso* cannot, and the universe that the speaker constructs conforms to the real viewpoint in the poem as Mazeppa's world view does not. This is not to suggest that the same messianic quality that we see in the other protagonists is not also an aspect of Dante; it clearly is, but it has not reached the degree recognized in the others, leaving this protagonist therefore a more trustworthy commentator on man's experience.

The poem is divided into four cantos, each of which constitutes the expression of a clear phase in the speaker's progression. The first contains the initial step in his emotional redemption, the admission of weakness and pain, which, though necessary, brings him perilously close to despair. In the second canto, imagining and foretelling a united Italy, Dante transcends the individual sense of loss he has described and thus demonstrates in this canto aspects of the prophetic powers to which he laid claim in the first. In the third canto he argues for the essentially prophetic and social function of the Poet. In the final canto he develops this argument to the point that represents both his intellectual conclusion and his emotional climax:

> I may not overleap the eternal bar
> Built up between us [Florence and himself], and will die alone,
>   Beholding with the dark eye of a Seer
>   The evil days to gifted souls foreshown,
> Foretelling them to those who will not hear;
>   As in the old time, till the hour be come
>   When Truth shall strike their eyes through many a tear,
> And make them own the Prophet in his tomb
>
> (IV, 147-54)

In the opening of the first canto the speaker reveals that, following the composition of the *Divina Commedia*, he has returned to "Man's frail world" and again feels "The weight of clay." [6] He is, he laments,

>   too soon bereft
>   Of the Immortal Vision which could heal
>   My earthly sorrows, and to God's own skies
>   Lift me from that deep Gulf without repeal,
>   Where late my ears rung with the damned cries
>   Of Souls in hopeless bale; and from that place
>   Of lesser torment, whence men may arise
>   Pure from the fire to join the Angelic race
>
> (I, 1-10)

The speaker has left the Vision imaging his own divine ideal and now must move from the World of Men toward a vision of the Self in terms of which he can live; or, put another way, he has ended the creation of the substance of his Work and must come to realize what the fact of that work personally means. By analogy the passage suggests two possibilities to him regarding his own present state: the infernal, which necessarily terminates in despair, or the purgatorial, whence he may rise pure to make the final affirmation in the poem. He begins appropriately with remembrance of Beatricē, who in his poem "led the mortal guest, / Unblasted by the Glory, though he trod / From star to star to reach the almighty throne." In life the image of Beatricē has from the first been the inspiration for all movement toward the Ideal ("Since my tenth sun gave summer to my sight / Thou wert my Life, the Essence of my thought, / Loved ere I knew the name of Love"), in terms of which he has derived the image of the matured Self, which must support his present evolution of the ideal of the Poet's art:

> they have not yet
> Quenched the old exile's spirit, stern and high.
> But the Sun, though not overcast, must set
> And the night cometh; I am old in days,
> And deeds, and contemplation, and have met
> Destruction face to face in all his ways.
> The World hath left me, what it found me, pure,
> And if I have not gathered yet its praise,
> I sought it not by any baser lure;
> Man wrongs, and Time avenges, and my name
> May form a monument not all obscure,
> Though such was not my Ambition's end or aim,
> To add to the vain-glorious list of those
> Who dabble in the pettiness of fame,
> And make men's fickle breath the wind that blows
> Their sail, and deem it glory to be classed
> With conquerors, and Virtue's other foes,
> In bloody chronicles of ages past.
> I would have had my Florence great and free;
> Oh Florence! Florence! unto me thou wast
> Like that Jerusalem which the Almighty He
> Wept over, "but thou wouldst not."

The theme of burial in Florence, introduced first in relation to Beatricē ("whose sweet limbs the sod / So long hath pressed, and the cold marble stone"), soon becomes crucial, recurring throughout the poem until its final development in the concluding stanza; at each recurrence it is indicative of the stage of the speaker's emotional progression. Continuing the apostrophe to Florence, clearly the new Jerusalem, Dante, accusing her of rejecting him as the adder that turns upon the breast that cherished it, recalls her sentence upon him, particularly that if he were to return, "this body [would be] forfeit to the fire." Echoing the purgatorial fire of the opening of the poem, the words at least suggest the speaker's essential belief in his own growth and purification through pain. But the process is neither immediate nor at this point complete; reflecting "how bitter is his country's curse / To him who *for* that country would expire, / But did not merit to expire *by* her," the speaker himself becomes bitter, then vindictive, foreseeing the time that Florence shall honor him and "be proud to have / The dust she dooms to scatter." But this he would reject: "No,—she denied me what was mine—my roof, / And shall not have what is not hers—my tomb." He plays with thoughts of power and revenge, deterred only by remembrance of Beatricē's own tomb in Florence: "My own Beatricē, I would hardly take / Vengeance upon the land which once was mine, / And still is hallowed by thy dust's return." Yet "my lone breast may burn / At times with evil feelings hot and harsh," he continues. "And sometimes the last pangs of a vile foe / Writhe in a dream before me, and o'erarch / My brows with hopes of triumph, —let them go!" He would, he protests, consciously reject the temptation which obviously appeals to him most graphically. Such hopes and dreams are "the last infirmities" of men "Who long have suffered more than mortal woe, / And yet being mortal still, have no repose / But on the pillow of

Revenge." Despite intellectual recognition of evil, he is emotionally drawn by the image to the point that, as he continues, he must admit this attraction:

> Revenge,
> Who sleeps to dream of blood, and waking glows
> With the oft-baffled, slakeless thirst of change,
> When we shall mount again, and they that trod
> Be trampled on, while Death and Até range
> O'er humbled heads and severed necks——Great God!
> Take these thoughts from me.

The moment of admission marks the emotional climax in the first canto of the poem.

The recognition of his vindictiveness is for the speaker the real beginning of his purge of this very hatred and of his ascent toward positive affirmation. Psychologically, however, the loss of such an emotional force as the hatred itself, albeit negative, leaves him for the moment extremely close to despair. Instantly recognizing the implications of his situation, the speaker turns to prayer: "to thy hands I yield / My many wrongs, and thine Almighty rod / Will fall on those who smote me,—be my Shield!" Obviously he is identifying the divine cause with his own, calling upon the God whose image he has lately fixed in his *Commedia* but who only at this time becomes for him a personal reality: "Even in that glorious Vision, which to see / And live was never granted until now, / And yet thou hast permitted this to me." He recalls his return to the real world from the ideal, the theme with which he has begun, an experience in itself potentially purgatorial:

> Alas! with what a weight upon my brow
>   The sense of earth and earthly things come back,
>   Corrosive passions, feelings dull and low,
> The heart's quick throb upon the mental rack,
>   Long day, and dreary night.

To justify himself as the Prophet of his own people Dante must dispose of the obvious fact of his present isolation from them. "I am not of this people, nor this age," he admits. Too long rejected by his people, "too long and deeply wrecked / On the lone rock of desolate Despair," he cannot now expect recognition by them during his remaining years. In this fact he finds the irony "Of spirits of my order . . . racked / In life," who "consume / Their days in endless strife, and die alone": only "Then [do] future thousands crowd around their tomb, / And pilgrims come from climes where they have known / The name of him—who now is but a name." But the achievement of posthumous fame in itself is emotionally meaningless for Dante; though in time he will feel fully the distinction, which he intellectually recognizes, between those who shall have merely fame and those who shall leave truth to their people, for the moment he finds the promise of fame small solace for the fact that he is "to wither thus—to tame / My mind down from its own infinity" rather than merely to die." He knows that in Florence even his sons, embittered by their mother, have rejected him. But this knowledge, though it brings "A bitter lesson," at least "leaves me free," one "made an Exile—not a Slave."

In the second canto, assuming "The Spirit of the fervent days of Old," Dante identifies himself with the land whose Prophet he claims to be. There is, then, a personal motivation (which in fulfilling he may transcend) for the speaker's apostrophe to Italy, in which, like the Hebrew Prophets to whom he has compared himself, Dante foretells sufferings, significantly resembling his own, that must come: "The Elements await but for the Word, / 'Let there be darkness!' and thou growst a tomb!" [7] They will offer sharp contrast to Italy's Edenic loveliness: "thou, so beautiful, shalt feel the sword, / Thou Italy! so fair that Paradise, / Revived in thee, blooms forth to man restored." The question is crucial: "Ah! must the sons of Adam lose it twice?" Looking from a point in time that is postlapsarian but occurs early in the history of his people, Dante foresees "The Goth . . . the German, Frank, and Hun." Despite similarities between Jerusalem and Florence, the present Italians, unlike the early Hebrews, appear to be unprotected by their God through Nature or their own will to survive. Once more Dante moves close to despair, but at a higher intellectual level, for it momentarily appears that he is to become the Prophet of a people rejected by God, therefore necessarily (though not intentionally) a false Prophet. Ultimately, however, he regards the people rather than their God as the cause; like all men, they are self-determining (otherwise Prophecy of any kind would have no place among them), possessing the power, as did the Hebrews of old, either to please or offend God, who remains always just and responds to them as they deserve. Their fault is disunity, a substitution of many standards for one that is somewhat reminiscent of the polygamy against which the monogamous Hebrew Prophets contended. The exhortation to unite becomes crucial to the future political survival of Italy and, in terms of this, therefore, to the present emotional survival of the speaker:

> Oh! my own beauteous land! so long laid low,
>   So long the grave of thy own children's hopes,
>   When there is but required a single blow
> To break the chain, yet—yet the Avenger stops,
>   And Doubt and Discord stept 'twixt thine and thee,
>   And join their strength to that which with thee copes;
> What is there wanting then to set thee free,
>   And show thy beauty in its fullest light?
>   To make the Alps impassable; and we,
> Her Sons, may do this with *one* deed——Unite.

Dante is messianic. But balancing between despair and over-confidence, he is, unlike the other protagonists we have seen, able, in his motion toward personal affirmation, to unite an inner world with an outer world that is real and meaningful.

Certitude characterizes the speaker at the opening of the third canto. "I cannot all record / That crowds on my prophetic eye," he remarks. "The Earth / And Ocean written o'er would not afford / Space for the annal, yet it shall go forth." From his apparent inner unity he has derived strength, which he would now impart to Italy. From his microcosm he imposes Value upon the macrocosm, and in so doing transcends his own situation with all of its pain, thereby more fully achieving that unity within the Self to which he has made claim.

Implying still that his are a wayward people and theirs an angry God, the speaker describes "the echoes of our groans . . . driven / Athwart the sound of archangelic songs" and pictures Italy in her suffering: "Like a harpstring stricken by the wind, / The sound of her lament shall, rising o'er / The Seraph voices, touch the Almighty Mind." As Prophet he brings to his people the truths they cannot know for themselves. Traditionally, the Prophet is also Poet, giving form to the people's lament. "To thee, my Country! whom before, as now / I loved and love," he dedicates himself: he "devote[s] the mournful lyre / And melancholy gift high Powers allow / To read the future." Once more recalling his late Vision, he regrets that his "fire / Is not as once it shone o'er thee" (though paradoxically, now fully affecting the Self, it shines more enduringly). In the *Commedia* he has described a world of death, toward which his view remained essentially that of an outsider; in his Prophecy for Italy, he foresees a world-to-be in life, of which he himself can have no part: "A Spirit forces me to see and speak, / And for my guerdon grants *not* to survive; / My heart shall be poured over thee [Italy] and break." Emotionally accepting the irony of his situation, Dante loses the personal Self in the Prophet's greater being.

Before continuing Italy's story, Dante recites the list of those ("the wise, / The gay, the learned, the generous, and the brave") who shall prefigure "The mortal Saviour who shall set thee free, / And see thy diadem, so changed and worn / By fresh barbarians, on thy brow replaced." He shall be anticipated by the "Poets [who] follow in the path I show, / And make it broader." Their songs, though varied, shall reflect Dante's own "Immortal Vision." He makes the necessary distinction between Poets and verse flatterers, those "too near the throne," thereby suggesting his rejection of the terms by which he could be buried in Florence and supporting his own position. In the train will come "out of the long file of sonneteers" some like Petrarch ("their Prince, [who] shall rank among my peers, / And Love shall be his torment"); Dante regards Ariosto and Tasso (not unexpectedly, in the light of their poetic scope and Tasso's imprisonment) as "two greater still" than Petrarch.[8] The speaker regards Tasso as one who is obviously part of the Prophet-Poet tradition: "his high harp / Shall, by the willow over Jordan's flood, / Revive a song of Sion." A degree of identity in their messianic roles is inevitable: "Such shall be his meek guerdon! who was sent / To be Christ's Laureate—they reward him well! / Florence dooms me but death or banishment."

The "penury and pain" which shall come to both Ariosto and Tasso pose the inevitable question to the speaker:

> Must all the finer thoughts, the thrilling sense,
> The electric blood with which their arteries run,
> Their body's self turned soul with the intense

> Feeling of that which is, and fancy of
> That which should be, to such a recompense
> Conduct? shall their bright plumage on the rough
> Storm be still scattered?

Implicit in his affirmative answer is the familiar proposition that the source of their power is divine: "formed of too penetrable stuff, / These birds of Paradise but long to flee / Back to their native mansion," for they are poisoned by "Earth's mist" and must "die or are degraded." There are, however, "some . . . who learned to bear, / Some whom no Power could ever force to droop," among whom he would place himself. He closes the canto with the figure comparing "The Alp's snow summit nearer heaven . . . seen" and "the Volcano's fierce eruptive crest," by which he dramatizes the fact that he, unlike the other Poets, has achieved serenity.

The contrast between real and potential Poets, with which Dante begins in the fourth canto, creates the opportunity that he needs to define Poetry. Those who might have become Poets but did not, the speaker proposes, "compressed / The God within them" and failed thereby at Self-realization:

> For what is Poesy but to create
> From overfeeling Good or Ill; and aim
> At an external life beyond our fate,
> And be the new Prometheus of new men,
> Bestowing fire from Heaven, and then, too late,
> Finding the pleasure given repaid with pain,
> And vultures to the heart of the bestower,
> Who, having lavished his high gift in vain,
> Lies chained to his lone rock by the sea-shore?
> So be it: we can bear
>
> (IV, 4-20)

The Poets themselves are those "Whose Intellect is an o'er-mastering Power / Which still recoils from its encumbering clay / Or lightens it to spirit." The essence of the Poets' work is divine: they are both Prophets and Priests, and their work transcends the limits of literature. Thus Dante can foresee Michelangelo as Poet, recreating the divine image in Moses and prophesying the Last Judgment: "The Stream of his great thoughts shall spring from me / The Ghibelline, who traversed the three realms / Which form the Empire of Eternity." And the Poets are necessarily opposed by tyrants, whose view of art is essentially mechanical rather than organic, "who but take her for a toy, / Emblems and monuments, and prostitute / Her charms to Pontiffs proud." The speaker once more asks why "the Sons of Fame," whose inspiration is divine, "Must pass their days in penury or pain, / Or step to grandeur through the paths of shame." Actually, he makes no answer, but in another apostrophe to Florence reaffirms his dedication and his sense of ultimate personal fulfillment:

> Florence! when this lone Spirit shall return
> To kindred Spirits, thou wilt feel my worth,
> And seek to honour with an empty urn
> The ashes thou shalt ne'er obtain—Alas!

The speaker now emotionally accepts the intellectual justification of his own "penury and pain," and he anticipates that time "When Truth shall strike their eyes through many a tear, / And make them own the Prophet in his tomb."

VII

Cain and Heaven and Earth

i

Cain, UNLIKE *Manfred,* IS PRINCIPALLY CONCERNED WITH THE conflict between good and evil. It offers no resolution, for by the very nature of the total point of view of the play, there is none to offer. The figure upon whom the intellectual question of the play is centered is, to a far more limited degree than Manfred, a total personality: he is largely a consciousness reacting to certain propositions but not so centrally involved as Manfred in the inner conflict between awareness and affirmation. Dominated by his sense of logic, he is moved, as only an absolutist can be moved, toward resolution of the conflict between apparent cosmic injustice and his own sense of right, between the image of his father's God and his own ideal of Good. There is of course to be no resolution. Unable to accept failure and at the same time overcome by the lack of reason manifest in his brother's sacrifice to a seemingly unjust God, Cain brings the first instance of death into the world, that of which he has heard but has been incapable of accepting within his own scheme of perfection. Though he shifts his intellectual position, from his own early absolutism toward Lucifer's cosmic relativism, he cannot make the emotional transition that this demands and in the end responds to the need for absolute action.

The first act is devoted almost entirely to Cain's problem: his need is to synthesize truth, beauty, and goodness, and then to reconcile these with the image of God that he has been given. The second act records his quest, by which he moves from an absolute fear that God determines the nature of Right to the relative notion that Right must precede God. The third act contains the working out of Cain's inevitable emotional failure to accept the essential ideas that his newly acquired knowledge has made necessary; in murdering Abel he unwillingly offers support for his father's belief in a just God who is opposed only by evil.

In the opening of the first act, Adam, Eve, Abel, Adah, and Zillah are, with the restrained participation of Cain, offering a sacrifice. The scene obviously foretells that in the third act, occurring at the end of Cain's journey. Following the prayers of those sacrificing, each of which (with what turns out to be unconscious irony) is directed toward God as the necessary cause of Good, Cain makes his position clear: since he must die, he refuses to thank God for life. To Eve such blasphemy as this is "The fruit of our forbidden tree." Adam, though now rejecting the intellectual quest, hovers stupidly at the edge of orthodoxy: "Oh God! why didst thou plant the tree of knowledge?" To Cain, however, their fault lay not in picking the fruit of the Tree of Knowledge but in forbearing to take that of the Tree of Life as well: "The snake spoke *truth;* it *was* the Tree of Knowledge; / It *was* the Tree of Life: knowledge is good, / And Life is good; and how can both be evil?" (I, i, 36-38) Eve recalls her own words at the Fall ("My boy! thou speakest as I spoke in sin, / Before thy birth"), unaware that Cain is moved by intellectual recognition of inconsistency rather than by vanity. "Content thee with what *is*," she urges, going forth with the others to their work.

Cain does not doubt the reality of such a God as envisaged by his father; rather, he rejects the idea that Good necessarily emerges from the Divine Being. The initial temptation of

Adam through "the Serpent and the woman" and his own consequent diminution demonstrate to him only that evil follows the will of God: "Because / He is all-powerful, must all-good, too, follow? / I judge but by the fruits—and they are bitter." Cain is now intellectually prepared for the appearance of Lucifer, a figure whose diminished beauty, though yoked with a kind of melancholy truth, seems to Cain himself to be removed from goodness.

Lucifer first denies that there is a real basis for Cain's fear that death is final: "Thou livest—and must live for ever. Think not / The Earth, which is thine outward cov'ring, is / Existence—it will cease—and thou wilt be." Applying the same reasoning to Lucifer that he has applied to God, Cain asks the figure before him if he is happy because he is great. Lucifer replies essentially that he is unhappy because he is conquered, and thus he cannot reign and create as does God. I am, he remarks, "One who aspired to be what made thee, and / Would not have made thee what thou art." He has strengthened Cain's doubts that God precedes Good, thereby making the initial intellectual identification between Cain and himself,

> Souls who dare use their immortality—
> Souls who dare look the Omnipotent tyrant in
> His everlasting face, and tell him that
> His evil is not good!

In the first place, Godhead appears limited: "If he made us— he cannot unmake: / We are immortal!" In the second, an evil creation postulates other than a good creator: "Goodness would not make / Evil; and what else hath he made?" In what resembles a parody of the essential picture in Neoplatonism, Lucifer images God flowing through unformed chaos, "Creating worlds, to make eternity / Less burthensome to his immense existence / And unparticipated solitude."

Misery is his essence and a necessary part of his creation, so that ultimately he must fail: "Let him crowd orb on orb: he is alone / Indefinite, Indissoluble Tyrant." Even were he to create "a Son unto himself—as he / Gave you a father," Lucifer concludes, "Mark me! that Son will be a sacrifice!"

The image of sacrifice reminds Cain, first of his own punishment for his father's sin, then of Abel, the "watching shepherd boy, who offers up / The firstlings of the flock to him who bids / The earth yield nothing to us without sweat." Cain is thus psychologically as well as intellectually receptive to Lucifer's arguments. "And hadst thou not been fit by thine own soul / For such companionship," Lucifer remarks, "I would not now / Have stood before thee as I am: a serpent / Had been enough to charm ye, as before." Unable to comprehend the intellectual implications of his position, Cain asks Lucifer if he were the serpent who tempted Eve. Lucifer's response, though appearing to be evasive in the question of his identity with the serpent, strikes at the heart of Adam's theological position, which is that innocent man can somehow be tempted and fall: "Did I plant things prohibited within / The reach of beings innocent, and curious / By their own innocence?" He reverts to an earlier suggestion: were he rather than the Godhead conqueror, he "would have made ye / Gods"; permitting Adam and Eve to take of the fruit of the Tree of Life, he "would / Have made ye live for ever, in the joy / And power of Knowledge." The proposition that life is essentially intellectual fundamentally denies the basis for Adam's belief in the Curse. At this point, however, Cain remains unable to understand it fully: he asks once more if Lucifer tempted his parents. Consistent with Lucifer's intellectual subjectivism ("Nothing can / Quench the mind, if the mind will be itself / And centre of surrounding things") is his reply:

> The snake *was* the snake—
> No more; and yet not less than those he tempted,
> In nature being earth also—*more* in *wisdom,*
> Since he could overcome them, and foreknew
> The knowledge fatal to their narrow joys.

The "Demon" to which the temptation is attributed in Adam's theology was an inner weakness in Man, in itself further evidence of the imperfection in Creation. Disobedience is implicit in earthly beings, needing in each case only sufficient stimulus, which, at the intellectual level, Lucifer now offers Cain. The life of the mind, however, could not exist for Cain apart from the "poor clay," so that, ironically, it must end in the actualization of the Death that has been foretold to Adam: Abel himself must become a sacrifice to Cain's "clay" rather than to his intellectual principle, to his created imperfection rather than to his Luciferian idealism.

To Lucifer's question, "Darest thou look on Death?" Cain's reply is anthropomorphic: "He has not yet / Been seen." He later remarks, "I thought it was a being: who could do / Such evil things to beings save a being?" The notion of extrinsic cause derived from Adam's theology which Cain accepts is, Lucifer proposes, a rationalization for intrinsic imperfection: Death is implicit in Life, destruction in creation, "the Destroyer" in "The Maker—Call him / Which name thou wilt: he makes but to destroy." Cain assents: "I knew not that, yet thought it, since I heard / Of Death: although I know not what it is— / Yet it seems horrible." Then, dreading Death, he ironically voices what is essentially a death wish ("Were I quiet earth, / There were no evil: would I ne'er had been / Aught else but dust!"), which Lucifer regards as "Less than thy father's—for he wished to know!" To Cain's question regarding Adam, "wherefore plucked he not / The Life-tree?" Lucifer responds, "He was hindered": only with real knowledge, such as Adam did not possess, can one achieve eternal life and destroy fear. It is this which Lucifer now offers, but only on condition (the full meaning of which Cain at this time necessarily cannot comprehend) that Cain "fall down and worship me—thy Lord." Reaffirming his devotion to the Godhead, Adam did not fulfill this condition, thereby illustrating the truth of Lucifer's earlier assertion that Adam was tempted by the serpent, to which his own physical imperfection responded, rather than by Lucifer representing the intellectual principle. In urging Cain's submission, Lucifer insists that he is distinct from the Godhead:

> I have nought in common with him!
> Nor would: I would be aught above—beneath—
> Aught save a sharer or a servant of
> His power. I dwell apart; but I am great:—
> Many there are who worship me, and more
> Who shall—be thou amongst the first.

With what is Lucifer's first suggestion of the essential Manichaean proposition he combines its traditional contradiction, the assertion that evil exists as privation of good: "Thou art my worshipper; not worshipping / Him makes thee mine the same." The seeming conflict between these positions is to be resolved (and from a traditional viewpoint, only partly) by Lucifer's later assertion that he, not the Godhead, is the spiritual principle.

Cain's momentary refusal to follow Lucifer on the pretext that he has promised to gather fruit for Abel's sacrifice is, he protests, evidence not of acceptance of Abel's theology but merely of his deference to "Abel's earnest prayer" and to Adah's tears. Adah enters and, unprepared, can find no difference between Lucifer and the angels she has already known. Cain gives the affirmation anticipated by Lucifer: "He is a God." But Adah, doubtful (for the serpent, too, spoke like a

God), implores Cain to abandon the Spirit, an act of which at this point he is intellectually incapable. Her assumption is that of her father, that knowledge brings sorrow, and proposes the contrary therefore of the Luciferian principle, that sorrow brings knowledge, "And Truth in its own essence cannot be / But good." Her rejection of the possibility that love such as hers and Cain's shall someday be regarded as evil dramatizes her conceptual incapacity: she cannot comprehend that her anthropomorphic image of Godhead or of Creation is not enduring and therefore less than perfect. And thus, after Lucifer's assertion that men are slaves imitating in their prayers the Godhead's creativity ("not from love, / But terror and self-hope"), Adah falls back, first upon the now familiar proposition that God precedes Right ("Omnipotence / Must be all goodness"), then upon simple emotional rejection: "Fiend! tempt me not with beauty; thou art fairer / Than was the Serpent, and as false." Adah emotionally recapitulates her mother's sin with the serpent:

> I cannot answer this immortal thing
> Which stands before me; I cannot abhor him;
> I look upon him with a pleasing fear,
> And yet I fly not from him: in his eye
> There is a fastening attraction which
> Fixes my fluttering eyes on his; my heart
> Beats quick; he awes me, and yet draws me near,
> Nearer and nearer:—Cain—Cain—save me from him!

Cain reassures her.

Adah, however, insists with ironic foresight that the knowledge that the Spirit brings will destroy love, an argument which Lucifer reduces to conclusions. "And if the higher knowledge quenches love, / What must *he be* you cannot love when known?" he asks. "Choose betwixt Love and Knowledge—since there is / No other choice: your sire hath chosen already: / His worship is but fear." Urged by Adah to "choose Love," Cain replies: "For thee, my Adah, I choose not—It was / Born with me—but I love nought else." Aware, nevertheless, of Man's inheritance, "agonies accumulated / By ages," Cain recognizes the fact that his love for Adah, by which the race shall be continued, is rendered absurd by the knowledge "that they are miserable" which Adam and his kind have received from the Tree of Knowledge. To Adah's wish that he be happy he replies, therefore, "Be thou happy, then, alone— / I will have nought to do with happiness, / Which humbles me and mine."

Adah's admission that solitary happiness is impossible is immediately seized upon by Lucifer and applied to her image of Godhead. To this Adah responds with the doctrine of creative Goodness, which by this point has become for Cain merely an Adamic inversion of the Luciferian assertion that Deity creates to escape the loneliness imposed by solitude. Queried by Lucifer about the reality of the Godhead, Adah argues from the existence of "his works" and their beauty, but the very being of Lucifer himself leads her into the dilemma which she necessarily cannot recognize: she has, she proposes, not seen God through his works,

> Save in my father, who is God's own image;
> Or in his angels, who are like to thee—
> And brighter, yet less beautiful and powerful
> In seeming: as the silent sunny noon,
> All light, they look upon us; but thou seem'st
> Like an ethereal night, where long white clouds
> Streak the deep purple, and unnumbered stars
> Spangle the wonderful mysterious vault
> With things that look as if they would be suns;
> So beautiful, unnumbered, and endearing,
> Not dazzling, and yet drawing us to them,
> They fill my eyes with tears, and so dost thou.

> Thou seem'st unhappy: do not make us so,
> And I will weep for thee.

But the essential irony of her suggestion arises from the fact that Lucifer is outside the need for finite love or compassion and requires only intellectual affirmation, which, in the case of Cain, must ultimately remain insufficient by reason of Cain's "poor clay," a fact in itself demonstrative of Lucifer's argument that Creation is essentially imperfect and therefore evil.

Lucifer leads Cain forth, promising Adah that he shall return within an hour: "With us acts are exempt from time, and we / Can crowd eternity into an hour, / Or stretch an hour into eternity." His qualifications remain meaningless to Adah, however, who regards time only as an image rather than as a concept. Lucifer's world, as he describes it in response to Adah's question ("Where dwellest thou?"), is that which the Manichaeans would attribute to the Godhead, the world of the intellect opposed to that of physical creation. It is clearly not that of the Serpent, then, recalled once more by Adah, for the Serpent belongs in reality to the physical principle, and only symbolically, relating to the intellectual quest, can it be associated with Lucifer. "If thou dost long for knowledge, I can satiate that thirst," Lucifer remarks to Cain, "nor [shall I] ask thee to partake of fruits / Which shall deprive thee of a single good / The Conqueror has left thee." Cain reaffirms his willingness, and they leave Adah alone and uncomprehending.

Adah's failure in the closing phase of the first act (against which Cain's limited readiness is set) has been, as Lucifer himself implies, her inability to distingush between myth and reality. In the first long speech in the second act, Lucifer explicitly rejects her world view, one composed of symbols taken literally:

Believe—and sink not! doubt and perish! thus
Would run the edict of the other God,
Who names me Demon to his angels; they
Echo the sound to miserable things,
Which, knowing nought beyond their shallow senses,
Worship the *word* which strikes their ear, and deem
Evil or good what is proclaimed to them
In their abasement. I will have none such:
Worship or worship not, thou shalt behold
The worlds beyond thy little world, nor be
Amerced for doubts beyond thy little life,
With torture of *my* dooming. There will come
An hour, when, tossed upon some water-drops,
A man shall say to a man, "Believe in me,
And walk the waters;" and the man shall walk
The billows and be safe. *I* will not say,
Believe in *me,* as a conditional creed
To save thee; but fly with me o'er the gulf
Of space an equal flight, and I will show
What thou dar'st not deny,—the history
Of past—and present, and of future worlds.

Lucifer requests intellectual susceptibility. Belonging to the
world of the flesh as much as to that of the mind, Cain will
feel the need to give emotional support, which Lucifer, by
his very nature, has not the capacity to receive. Herein lies
the cause for what is to become Cain's tragedy. Essentially, as
Lucifer has insisted from the time of his first appearance
before Cain, power does not imply Truth or Goodness; God
does not precede Right, and Cain belongs in part at least
to the Godhead. Though Lucifer can intellectually accept the
proposition that imperfection is meaningful (that his struggle
with the physical principle is never to be concluded), to Cain
the idea can never become an emotional reality. His physical,
and therefore emotional, being demands an image bound by

time and space. Thus death slowly emerges in Cain's consciousness as a beneficent force, made meaningful as Lucifer's arguments erode Cain's underlying belief in universal anthropocentricity and in preservation of self and kind:

> Spirit! I
> Know nought of Death, save as a dreadful thing
> Of which I have heard my parents speak, as of
> A hideous heritage I owe to them
> No less than life—a heritage not happy,
> If I may judge, till now. But, Spirit! if
> It be as thou hast said (And I within
> Feel the prophetic torture of its truth),
> Here let me die: for to give birth to those
> Who can but suffer many years, and die—
> Methinks is merely propagating Death,
> And multiplying murder.

The image of death that Cain now holds contrasts with that of which "The Other / Spake . . . unto my father, when / He shut him forth from Paradise" (in terms of Lucifer's argument, this is necessarily total death, since "The Other" as the physical principle could control nothing beyond the body). "But at least / Let what is mortal of me perish," Cain concludes, "that / I may be in the rest as angels are." Recognizing the necessary immortality of his own intellectual being, Cain can now give an affirmation to Lucifer such as, among men, he has been unable to give to God. Before Cain returns to earth, as he must do, Lucifer leads him to the Luciferian realm, that of the Ideal, "The phantasm of the world; of which thy world / Is but the wreck." It is the region of the mind, of the dark light that is comprehensible but beyond the reach of the senses, refuting the absolutism of the limited view of the earthbound.

In the second scene, set in Hades, Lucifer renders death

present and real to Cain's view. First cursing God and his
father for placing death in Man's world, Cain slowly comes
to full awareness of the other life which God has not revealed
to Adam, represented by those beings now around him, who

> bear not
> The wing of Seraph, nor the face of man,
> Nor form of mightiest brute, nor aught that is
> Now breathing; mighty yet and beautiful
> As the most beautiful and mighty which
> Live, and yet so unlike them, that I scarce
> Can call them living.

These, the phantasms of the pre-Adamite creatures of earth,
were made and destroyed in terms of the needs of the Godhead; superior to the race of Adam, they imply diminution of
the Creator's power. With them, Lucifer asserts, Cain has
only life and death in common; otherwise, Cain's attributes
are animal, characteristic of "Things whose enjoyment was to
be in blindness— / A Paradise of Ignorance, from which /
Knowledge was barred as poison."

Cain now rejects earth, remarking, "I rather would remain;
I am sick of all / That dust has shown me—let me dwell in
shadows." Within the dichotomous structure of the universe,
however, though Lucifer can liberate him intellectually, the
other principle, the creative Godhead, expresses itself only
materially, and Cain, belonging in part to it, must return to
earth to live and, before he can return to the Luciferian
realm, to die. Death, like physical life, is a condition imposed
upon Man by the Creator. Hence, Lucifer, moving toward a
concern with the nature of the effects of the Fall of Man, now
explains:

> thou now beholdest as
> A vision that which is reality

To make thyself fit for this dwelling, thou
Must pass through what the things thou seest have passed—
The gates of Death.

Though clearly Death had been present in the pre-Adamite
world, the Fall brought Death to Man. Though the Tree
brought no direct knowledge, "It may be death leads to the
highest knowledge," Lucifer points out, "And being of all
things the sole thing certain, / At least leads to the *surest*
science." Only in this sense, that it provided the means by
which the intellect of each man might eventually be released
from the burden imposed by Creation, could the Fall be
regarded (in the way that the Adamites must regard it in
order to justify it) as fortunate: "therefore / The Tree was
true, though deadly." Self-centered and literal, Man has accepted the Creator of matter as all, his own death as final.
Beyond this point Cain has now moved, accepting the possibility of eternal intellectual life, but he does not really (and
before death, cannot) comprehend the nature of "These dim
realms! I see them, but I know them not."

Bound by an awareness and a certain fundamental emotional acceptance of the conditions imposed upon Man by
physical creation, Cain is disturbed by the seeming paradox
that Man's death is requisite to his full intellectual freedom,
that only through sorrow can Truth lead to Goodness. Allowing emotional activity to pass for intellectual activity, he
rejects the Luciferian proposition that evil is "A part of all
things" on the basis that he himself, a part of creation,
"thirst[s] for good." "And who and what doth not?" Lucifer
replies. "*Who* covets evil / For its own bitter sake?—*None*—
nothing! 'tis / The leaven of all life, and lifelessness." Cain
believes that he finds Goodness in life through Beauty (Adah
is his principal example), but this, Lucifer argues, is delusion,
for Beauty in Life must in time yield to Death. To Cain

Lucifer's argument poses the fundamental question of the reason for life, which Cain as Man is emotionally constrained to ask. He has been unable to comprehend Lucifer's explanation, made in terms of "The Other," the creative, principle; and in using the parable of the stricken lamb to reject the paradox of a fortunate fall, which Adam has urged in justification of what Cain now recognizes as the imperfection of Creation, Cain fails to recognize how fully the implications of his rejection support Lucifer's explanation:

> but I thought, that 'twere
> A better portion for the animal
> Never to have been *stung at all,* than to
> Purchase renewal of its little life
> With agonies unutterable, though
> Dispelled by antidotes.

Cain still protests that Love itself brings Good, pitying Lucifer, who seems to love none. He regards Death as both the antithesis and the corollary of Life, but his view is that of the absolutist and does not comprehend the effects of time in diminishing Beauty, at the level at which he has experienced it, and in leading toward Death.

Lucifer now remarks that Abel seems to find favor in the eyes of Adam and Jehovah. Cain, struck by hearing the doubts that he has felt, makes his final attempt to repudiate Lucifer:

> Spirit!
> *Here* we are in *thy* world; speak not of *mine.*
> Thou hast shown me wonders: thou hast shown me those
> Mighty Pre-Adamites who walked the earth
> Of which ours is the wreck: thou hast pointed out
> Myriads of starry worlds, of which our own
> Is the dim and remote companion, in
> Infinity of life: thou hast shown me shadows

Of that existence with the dreaded name
Which my sire brought us—Death; thou hast shown me much
But not all: show me where Jehovah dwells,
In his especial Paradise—or *thine:*
Where is it?

To Lucifer's reply, "*Here,* and o'er all space," Cain objects,
for his intellectual activity is conditioned by images bound
by time and space: "But ye / Have some allotted dwelling—
as all things." He concludes as he must, that Jehovah and
Lucifer share a dwelling. "No, we reign / Together," Lucifer
replies, "but our dwellings are asunder." To Cain's suggestion
that unity would prevail if only one reigned or both reigned
in harmony, Lucifer, pointedly using the analogy of two
brothers which Cain has put forth and applying it to Cain and
Abel, makes the essential assertion that both reign as "the
two Principles." As an absolutist Cain comprehends this only
with the qualification that one must be, from the human
viewpoint, evil. Lucifer rejects the suggestion that this is he.
To do Man good in terms that are comprehensible by Man
is the task for Man's Creator: "*I* made ye not; / Ye are *his*
creatures, and not mine." In his final speeches, made as he
prepares to lead Cain physically back to earth, Lucifer,
echoing his own refutation of the idea that the Godhead
determines the nature of Goodness, explains that in conflict Jehovah and he represent two eternal and indestructible
forces, paradoxically in deadly antithesis:

> He as a conqueror will call the conquered
> *Evil;* but what will be the *Good* he gives?
> Were I the victor, *his* works would be deemed
> The only evil ones.

Lucifer's position is essentially one that retains the central
dichotomy but reverses the terms of the Manichaean thesis:

Lucifer represents the intellectual and ideal Principle, and the Godhead the material Principle.[1] Lucifer now pursues to its conclusions the argument from design, which as the basis of much of Adam's teaching is most familiar perhaps to Cain:

> Evil and Good are things in their own essence,
> And not made good or evil by the Giver;
> But if he gives you good—so call him; if
> Evil springs from *him,* do not name it *mine,*
> Till ye know better its true fount; and judge
> Not by words, though of Spirits, but the fruits
> Of your existence, such as it must be.

His final assertion, based upon his doctrine of the two Principles, is subjectivist in its conclusions:

> *One good* gift has the fatal apple given,—
> Your *reason:*—let it not be overswayed
> By tyrannous threats to force you into faith
> 'Gainst all external sense and inward feeling:
> Think and endure,—and form an inner world
> In your own bosom—where the outward fails;
> So shall you nearer be the spiritual
> Nature, and war triumphant with your own.

The irony of Cain's position, which is to be dramatized in the third act, arises from the fact that his "poor clay" renders him unable to "Think and endure" despite the intellectual motivation that Lucifer might have given him. In his encounter with Abel, his emotional and therefore material aspect, given him by the material Principle, asserts itself, and he kills Abel. The direct temptation to do so would seem (in terms of the Luciferian cosmogony, which, in the absence of any other, must condition the intellectual reaction to situations in the play) not to have come from Lucifer, who only teaches intellectual defiance, but rather from Cain's own created weakness. If Lucifer has been the giver of Truth to Cain, then the act of murder must recall and illustrate, with some degree of irony, Lucifer's recent pronouncement: "Evil and Good are things in their own essence, / And not made good or evil by the Giver."

In the setting of the opening of the third act, explicitly reminiscent of that in the first, Cain and Adah are together near Eden. It is apparent that, following his intense intellectual experience, Cain has fallen into a kind of despair. He addresses his sleeping son, Enoch, foretelling more than he understands:

> He must dream—
> Of what? Of Paradise! Aye! dream of it,
> My disinherited boy! 'Tis but a dream;
> For never more thyself, thy sons, nor fathers,
> Shall walk in that forbidden place of joy!

Adah, uncomprehending, is distressed though grateful to the "proud Spirit," "that he so soon / Hath given thee back to us." The ironic error in her position becomes progressively more apparent in their discussion of the time of his absence: to Adah time is fixed and absolute, measured by the sun, which is itself part of Creation and thereby the work of the material Principle; to Cain time is subjective ("The mind then hath capacity of time, / And measures it by that which it beholds, / Pleasing or painful; little or almighty") and, so far as its subjectivity is intellectual rather than emotional, an aspect of the realm of the alternate Principle in the universal dichotomy. In this viewpoint and in his recognition of his own "littleness," Cain demonstrates that to the degree possible for Man he has come to accept Lucifer's cosmic relativism. Adah attempts to change his position, urging first the paradox of *felix cupla* and then the doctrine of vicarious atonement, both of which Cain rejects as evidence only of a bestial Deity, "the Insatiable of life."

Approaching the two altars prepared by Abel, Cain recalls Lucifer's remarks upon the content of worship: Abel's "base humility / Shows more of fear than worship—as a bribe / To the Creator." Cain's suggestion that he kill the sleeping Enoch rather than to have him live in pain is merely a dramatization of the conclusions of his rejection of Adah's belief in the beneficence of Creation, foretelling of course the death of Abel. As Enoch awakens, Adah pleads only for Cain's love for them, which has become, in the light of Cain's newly acquired but hardly assimilated knowledge, intellectually purposeless. Abel appears, and he and Cain are soon left alone.

The sacrifice scene recalls that of the first act and points toward the heart of the philosophic difference between the brothers, the question of the validity of cosmic Evil serving the end of cosmic Good. Abel's prayer expectedly reveals his firm belief that Godhead necessarily precedes and determines the nature of Good. Cain's, ironically carrying Abel's assumptions to their personal conclusions, echoes Lucifer's remarks:

> all
> Rests upon thee; and Good and Evil seem
> To have no power themselves, save in thy will—
> And whether they be good or ill I know not,
> Not being omnipotent, nor fit to judge
> Omnipotence—but merely to endure
> Its mandate; which thus far I have endured.

The whirlwind scattering Cain's offering is for Abel emblematic but for Cain merely phenomenal. The quarrel that follows centers upon the question of the justice of sacrifice and ends with the sacrifice of Abel: Cain's half-assimilated Luciferian knowledge and his own growing wish for death have come together in a moment in which his irrational "poor clay" moves him to defy Lucifer's final exhortation. Cain, who has seen only the spiritual effects of death, now witnesses it as a physical reality, an expression of the creative Principle in the universe rather than directly as the liberator of the intellectual spirit. The impact of his deed is entirely emotional: "This is a vision, else I am become / The native of another and worse world. / The earth swims round me."

Following Zillah's frenzied scream, of which the horror is perhaps intensified by its ironic obviousness, "Father!— Eve!— / Adah!—come hither! Death is in the world!" Cain, left alone, remarks:

> And who hath brought him there?—I—who abhor
> The name of Death so deeply, that the thought
> Empoisoned all my life, before I knew
> His aspect—I have led him here, and given
> My brother to his cold and still embrace,
> As if he would not have asserted his
> Inexorable claim without my aid.

Moved by his act of flesh, Cain now repudiates what Lucifer has taught him: "I am awake at last—a dreary dream / Had maddened me;—but *he* shall ne'er awake!" The denouement, appropriately rapid, follows, ending in paradox. Cain, who has come to conceive of Death as an aspect of the realm of the material Principle which nevertheless is the instrument for Man's release to the intellectual Principle, is doomed to wander forth, "a fugitive . . . / . . . and vagabond on earth," marked for Life rather than for Death.

ii

Heaven and Earth, though supposedly incomplete,[2] may be regarded in its present form as a structural whole. It is composed of three scenes, of which the first two, though quite brief, establish as characters, respectively, the female descendants of Cain and the family of Noah. In the third scene, the problem, particularly as it has developed in the consciousness of Japhet, is resolved. The characters fall into pairs: Samiasa and Azaziel, the angels; Irad and Japhet, the men; Aholibamah and Anah, the Cainite women in love with the angels; finally the spokesmen for God, the Archangel Raphael and Noah. Of these the angels are indistinguishable as personalities, and Irad soon drops from the action. Japhet remains as the protagonist, one whose consciousness is most crucially affected by the divine acts. Aholibamah and Anah act out defiance and submission, respectively, a fact that becomes crucial as the central concern in the play develops, Election and human reward. Raphael, obviously more sophisticated than Noah, makes theological pronouncements which Noah, to the limit of his capacities, reflects. What they say offers a guide to the apparent universal framework within which human action occurs.

Though *Heaven and Earth* is frequently compared with *Cain*,[3] there is but limited intellectual similarity. *Cain* questions the validity and thereby the truth of the essential Hebraic-Christian theodicy. *Heaven and Earth,* far more restricted in both its subject and implications, is certainly simpler in both its structure and its arguments. The principal intellectual concern of the drama, the justice of Divine Election, never is made the object of an exhaustive inquiry. The total viewpoint is clearly anti-Calvinistic,[4] but despite assertion and dramatization, it is not insistently so; near the conclusion, Japhet, without excessive difficulty though little conviction, can accede to his father's wishes and accept the reality, if not the justice, of his father's cosmogony.

The opening scene establishes, first the nature of the relation of the angels Azaziel and Samiasa to Anah and

Aholibamah, secondly the personal differences in the characters of the submissive Anah and the proud Aholibamah. In
the second scene Irad and Japhet appear, the one simply to
set forth the personality and problem of the other. Japhet
is in love with Anah, but she rejects him. He combines
intellectual curiosity with a naïve unwillingness to accept the
fact about Anah which Irad can believe regarding Aholibamah, that she is in love with another. Despite his belief
(that she "but loves her God"), Japhet concedes that she
does not love him, but *he* continues to love *her*. It is clearly
important to the later action that the relation be firmly
established early in the play: Anah, the emotionally submissive sister, would seem to deserve the salvation which
Heaven is to deny her, whereas Japhet, one who is elect,
remains, at least until Anah's disappearance, intellectually
defiant, questioning the apparent injustice in the case of one
he loves.

In his soliloquy following Irad's departure, Japhet, lament-
ing the failure of love, remarks upon the "many signs and
portents [which] have proclaimed / A change at hand, and an
o'erwhelming doom / To perishable beings." He prays that
Anah might be spared God's wrath, and so first indicates his
essential disbelief in, and failure to understand, the inflexibility of the Divine Will, the conclusion of the thesis that
God precedes Right. Such is to become the basis of Japhet's
intellectual and emotional problem in the ensuing action;
but in terms of the theology of his father, constructed upon
an absolute acceptance of the proposition of Divine inflexibility, Japhet's problem is only emotional, for mind cannot
affect what is fixed. Thus he is *to appear* to have (but not in
reality to have, since he is elect) the choice between continuing, and necessarily fatal, defiance or submission.

After the close of Japhet's soliloquy and his departure,
Noah and his son Shem appear. Told by Shem that Japhet

has probably gone to Anah's tents, Noah makes the first proclamation of the foreordained destruction of the Cainites. Japhet, he remarks,

> Still loves this daughter of a fated race,
> Although he could not wed her if she loved him,
> And that she doth not. Oh, the unhappy hearts
> Of men! that one of my blood, knowing well
> The destiny and evil of these days,
> And that the hour approacheth, should indulge
> In such forbidden yearnings!

To Shem's plea that Noah not search for Japhet and thereby expose himself to danger, Noah replies by asserting his own election: "Do not fear for me: / All evil things are powerless on the man / Selected by Jehovah." He foretells the nature of the action in the third scene, the way by which Japhet, who has seemingly fallen into doubt and toward intellectual despair, is, as one of the elect, actually recalled and, filled with Divine Grace, made to merit the salvation that has consistently been intended for him; the irony underlying all action in the final phase of the drama arises from the fact that, despite all appearances, Japhet cannot sin, and all apparent sin must be taken merely as a false sign which will lead toward sin those who are not elect.

In the opening of the third scene, Japhet, standing at the mouth of a cavern in the Caucasus, foresees the destruction by the Flood of what he has known of Nature—and of the Cainites. He does not question either the existence or the power of the predestining God, but he begins to have doubts about the essential justice of predestination itself: "My kinsmen, / Alas! what am I better than ye are, / That I must live beyond ye?" It is to him emotionally unacceptable that death must come to "all things, save . . . us, / And the predestined creeping things reserved / By my sire to Jehovah's bidding."

The contradictions involved, particularly felt by him with regard to Anah, are inexplicable in terms of all that his association with Nature and Beauty has seemed to teach him:

>   May
>   *He* [Noah] preserve *them*, and I *not* have the power
>   To snatch the loveliest of earth's daughters from
>   A doom which even some serpent, with his mate,
>   Shall 'scape to save his kind to be prolonged,
>   To hiss and sting through some emerging world,
>   Reeking and dank from out the slime.

He approaches the point of asserting that predestination is the instrument of destruction and evil rather than of creativity and good:

>   All beauteous world!
>   So young, so marked out for destruction, I
>   With a cleft heart look on thee day by day,
>   And night by night, thy numbered days and nights.
>   I cannot save thee, cannot save even her
>   Whose love had made me love thee more; but as
>   A portion of thy dust, I cannot think
>   Upon thy coming doom without a feeling
>   Such as—Oh God! and canst thou—

The Spirit now appearing before Japhet, followed later by others of his kind, obviously emphasizes the conclusions of Japhet's suggestions (all might, therefore, be regarded as projectional), that life without the strength to resist or physical salvation without intellectual purpose is merely an ironic gift of the creative-destructive Deity. By saving Japhet's life for him, the Spirit proposes, Noah only preserves the evil and pain of that life. The Spirit tries to tempt Japhet toward Despair, which, if real, would be sin indicating that, despite words and other signs, he is not actually among the elect. "Son of the saved!" intones the Spirit,

> When thou and thine have braved
> The wide and warring element;
> When the great barrier of the deep is rent,
> Shall thou and thine be good or happy?—No!
> Thy new world and new race shall be of woe—
> Less goodly in their aspect, in their years
> Less than the glorious giants, who
> Yet walk the world in pride,
> The Sons of Heaven by many a mortal bride.
> Thine shall be nothing of the past, save tears!
> And art thou not ashamed
> Thus to survive,
> And eat, and drink, and wive?
> With a base heart so far subdued and tamed,
> As even to hear this wide destruction named,
> Without such grief and courage, as should rather
> Bid thee await the world-dissolving wave,
> Than seek a shelter with thy favoured father,
> And build thy city o'er the drowned earth's grave?
> Who would outlive their kind,
> Except the base and blind?

The Chorus of Spirits now speaks, anticipating the Chorus of Mortals, which appears at the end of the scene to dramatize the truth of the Spirits' assertion, that a "prayer-exacting Lord, / To whom the omission of a sacrifice / Is vice," is responsible for creation, a process often repeated and intrinsically evil. Interrupting the Chorus, Japhet repudiates its suggestions, with the argument that Providential Good expresses itself ultimately through a paradox, that out of evil greater good to Man must come. The point at issue is the reality of the relation between Heaven and Earth. Though the reality must be unquestioned, Japhet proposes, the nature of the relation is comprehended only by God but will in time be revealed to Man. The implications, which crucially apply to Japhet, remain unexpressed by him: if God's ways seem to Man unjust, then Man's reason is deficient. The Spirit, moved by his own sense of powerlessness rather than by recognition of God's justice, accepts Japhet's prophecy of the Redeemer with only the qualification, "Meantime still struggle in the mortal chain, / Till Earth wax hoary; / War with yourselves, and Hell, and Heaven, in vain." The Chorus reemerges, foretelling the Flood, the destruction of the Cainites, and the election of the seed of Seth.

Momentarily alone, Japhet questions the comprehensibility, at least in terms of time and space, of the prophecy:

> Aye, day will rise; but upon what?—a chaos,
> Which was ere day; and which, renewed, makes Time
> Nothing! for, without life, what are the hours?
> No more to dust than is Eternity
> Unto Jehovah, who created both.
> Without him, even Eternity would be
> A void: without man, Time, as made for man,
> Dies with man, and is swallowed in that deep
> Which has no fountain; as his race will be
> Devoured by that which drowns his infant world.

The sight of Anah with the angel Azaziel apparently leads Japhet further in the direction of Despair, suggested by his intellectual doubts and urged upon him by the Spirit. The woman and the angel represent to him the wrong kind of relation between Heaven and Earth, both theologically (Man is put "Upon the earth to toil and die; and they [the angels] / Are made to minister on high unto / The Highest") and personally ("Anah! Anah! my / In vain, and long, and still to be,

beloved! / Why walk'st thou with this Spirit[?]"). Though
Anah's love for the errant angel can be regarded theologically
as a sign of her foreordained damnation, which she is now
simply justifying, her presence and the apparently good impulses which direct her give emotional emphasis to Japhet's
doubts of the justice of predestination. Only Aholibamah
clearly dramatizes her own reprobation:

> And dost thou think that we,
> With Cain's, the eldest born of Adam's, blood
> Warm in our veins,—strong Cain! who was begotten
> In Paradise,—would mingle with Seth's children?
> Seth, the last offspring of old Adam's dotage?
> No, not to save all Earth, were Earth in peril!
> Our race hath always dwelt apart from thine
> From the beginning, and shall do so ever.

Though the irony in Aholibamah's position is obvious to
Japhet, the involvement of Anah in it moves him to regard
her words with a helpless seriousness. Cain, their "father's
father," was, she boasts, "The eldest born of man, the strong-
est, bravest, / And most enduring," one who passed his qualities to his children: "Look upon / Our race; behold their
stature and their beauty, / Their courage, strength, and
length of days." That Anah does not share her sister's resist-
ance to the will of God ("Whate'er our God decrees, / The
God of Seth as Cain, I must obey, / And will endeavour patiently to obey") and that she is totally non-Cainite in her
sibling love ("Aholibamah! / Oh! if there should be mercy
—seek it, find it: / I abhor Death, because that thou must
die") simply intensify Japhet's intellectual awareness of apparent inconsistency in the Divine scheme, so that, after
Aholibamah's affirmation of "a God of Love, not Sorrow," he

remarks: "Alas! what else is Love but Sorrow? Even / He who made earth in love had soon to grieve / Above its first and best inhabitants." Japhet has thus attributed finite qualities, sorrow and perhaps flexibility of the will, to God, a fact which in itself would seem to be reason for, or evidence of, reprobation. But Japhet is elect and, within the universal structure, all indications to the contrary must really be seen as false signs, designed to lead into perdition those who have been damned from all eternity.

Noah, the instrument of predestination, appears with Shem. His mission would appear to be to recall his son to an emotional and intellectual position acceptable in God's sight, but for the moment he is intent upon arguing that the association of angels and women "Cannot be good": such was not meant to be, and the angels, in their association, appear to be attempting to circumvent the will of God, whose essential quality in Noah's view is His inflexibility rather than His union of what Man would regard as Beauty, Truth, and Goodness:

> Not ye [the angels] in all your glory can redeem
> What he who made you glorious hath condemned.
> Were your immortal mission safety, 'twould
> Be general, not for two, though beautiful;
> And beautiful they are, but not the less
> Condemned.

That Noah talks, as has been suggested, "like a street-preacher," [5] is undeniable, but that he clearly should do so has somehow not been emphasized. Noah represents a kind of simple certitude, against which the doubts of Japhet are set. The contrast is structurally essential. Japhet has reached the emotional climax to which his love for Anah, interacting with his intellectual doubt, has led him:

Noah.   Son! Son!
If that thou would'st avoid their doom, forget
That they exist: they soon shall cease to be,
While thou shalt be the sire of a new world,
And better

Japh.   Let me die with *this,* and *them!*

Forced into the position of defending his cosmogony, Noah
argues that for the elect no sin is possible: "Thou *shouldst*
for such a thought, but shalt not: he / Who *can,* redeems
thee." And in so doing, he implies the proposition which remains unacceptable to Japhet, that those who are reprobate
can do nothing to merit salvation, of which the essential justice is questioned by Samiasa: "And why him and thee, /
More than what he, thy son, prefers to both?" In his answer
Noah echoes Japhet's earlier argument that Man alone frequently lacks the capacity to understand God's ways when
they seem unjust and must depend on revelation: "Ask him
who made thee greater than myself / And mine, but not less
subject to his own almightiness.'

Noah appeared at the moment that Japhet approached
Despair; the Archangel Raphael now arrives as Noah seems
to be moving toward a theological impasse. In coming partly
to impose "Jehovah's *late* decree" (italics mine) that angels
no longer walk the earth, Raphael ironically suggests the
mutability of Divine will. To Azaziel's question, "Dost thou
not err as we / In being here?" his response is teleological.
He confirms for the angels the prophecy of the Flood, urging
them to return while there is time. He himself, however, falls
momentarily close to doubt, asking the reason that "this
Earth [cannot] be made, or be destroyed, / Without involving ever some vast void / In the immortal ranks." Satan,
whose image Raphael invokes as a warning to the angels of

the fruit of rebellion, becomes for Raphael an object of brief regret, leading ultimately to the wish, admittedly "impious": "Would the hour / in which he fell could ever be forgiven!" But Raphael returns to his directed purpose, unscathed by seeming impiety because he is elect. "Satan," he remarks to Azaziel and Samiasa, "cannot tempt / The angels, from his further snares exempt." But in woman reside the sin and the power to tempt, and in these women, made reprobate by God, destruction is implicit.

Aholibamah, moved by Raphael's insistence upon the inevitability of the destruction of the race of Cain, assumes the position that is essentially Cainitic, an ironic acceptance in this instance of the will of God and a resignation therefore to death. Anah, like Aholibamah, gives up her angelic lover, but selflessly, that he "shalt not suffer woe / For me." The obvious contrast moves Japhet once more toward Despair: he asks his father to intervene on behalf of these Cainite women, or at least to permit Japhet himself to die. Asserting that either course would represent an attempt to circumvent the will of God, Noah carries his belief in Divine precedence over Good toward what might constitute a dilemma: to ask God to alter a Divine proclamation for Man would be to "have God commit a sin for thee." Japhet, apparently forced by this to the point of decision, reverses the precedence to which his father subscribes: "Oh God! be thou a God, and spare / Yet while 'tis time!" He is silenced by Noah, who asks forgiveness from Raphael for Japhet's "fond despair."

Ordered by Raphael to return, the angels ("Who are, or should be, passionless and pure") refuse, thereby demonstrating that they have been reprobate from the beginning, a fact now emphasized by archangelic decree: "Then from this hour, / [Be] Shorn as ye are of all celestial power, / And aliens from your God." As the cry of sea birds rises and the "better light" of the sun disappears, Japhet is driven toward total rejection: he refuses to leave Anah and is damned by Noah. But Raphael intervenes, reiterating the essential teaching that Noah as mere Man has been unable to sustain beyond the point of emotional equilibrium, that as one among the elect Japhet cannot damn himself:

> Thy son, despite his folly, shall not sink:
> He knows not what he says, yet shall not drink
>   With sobs the salt foam of the swelling waters;
> But be, when passion passeth, good as thou,
>   Nor perish like Heaven's children with man's daughters.

Denouement is rapid. "Heaven and earth unite / For the annihilation of all life," Aholibamah remarks. "Unequal is the strife / Between our strength and the Eternal Might!" The external struggle ceases to be qualitative, concerned with the relation of God to Right, and becomes merely quantitative. "The moment cometh to approve thy strength; / And learn at length / How vain to war with what thy God commands," Raphael tells Azaziel, "Thy former force was in thy faith." The fleeing Mortals in a Chorus invoke Divine justice as the flood rises, intensifying thereby the irony in their position. Anah and Aholibamah fly off with the angels. Japhet, resigned to his loss of Anah, submits to the will of his father and thereby of his God. The Chorus of Mortals asks him how he can now sit "safe amidst the elemental strife"; however, without Anah, he is unmoved, even by the woman offering him her infant that he might save it. "Peace!" he replies, rejecting what his intellectual questions (which, in Anah's absence, are no longer motivated) have taught him, " 'tis no hour for curses, but for prayer!"

The Mortals in Chorus, though at first appearing not to deserve their fate, are moved in anger to curse God and thus to justify His curse upon them. Only one Mortal holds against all others, accepting the Divine decree: "He gave me life—he taketh but / The breath which is his own." This represents the absolute affirmation, achieved through the negation of Self and the denial of Mind, but in the light of Japhet's earlier struggle it is ultimately ironic. And the irony is intensified at the close of the play, in which, with the waters rising around him, Japhet is still unable to give emotional acceptance to the Divine decree that, with all perishing about him, he must live.

VIII

Beppo and
the Structure of *Don Juan*

i

THOUGH FOR BOTH HISTORICAL[1] AND CRITICAL REASONS *Beppo*
and *Don Juan* traditionally fall together in a consideration
of Byron's poetry, there are significant differences between
the two poems. Of these, length and narrative completeness
are most obvious. Equally important is the relative structural
complexity, particularly as this is determined in each poem
by the nature of the speaker. In *Beppo* he appears to be one,
but in *Don Juan* an indefinite many, whose elements kaleido-
scopically fall together in an unending sequence so that iden-
tical forms never seem quite to reoccur.

The speaker in *Beppo,* though a single figure, is nevertheless an ironic one, whose naïveté and simplicity clash sharply
with the nature of the story he is going to tell. At best his
protagonist ("His name Giuseppe, called more briefly 'Beppo'") is the least significant of the three principals; the story
is really about only Beppo's wife and her lover, the Count.
Of this fact the speaker appears to be unaware; similarly, he
seems not to know that for the most part his narrative is lost
among his digressions. Set in the pre-Lenten Venetian Carnival (during which period in "All countries of the Catholic
persuasion," we are told, "The People take their fill of recrea-
tion"), the story concerns indulgence and abstinence. The

167

speaker appears to regard his materials literally and to be unable to recognize the clear association between two kinds of appetite, so that when he prepares to tell his story and for this purpose discusses the reasons for the Carnival, he seems to be totally unaware of the ambiguities which his description involves. Naïvely he employs terms and phrases which have (certainly for the early nineteenth-century Englishman) sexual as well as other significance.[2] We need not pursue the question, but we should remain aware, as many critics have failed or been unwilling to do, that this is part of the activity in the poem, particularly during the early stanzas. Sexuality is clearly a major theme in *Beppo,* but it is treated with no more direct seriousness than that with which Beppo himself is regarded as the protagonist or Italian society (rather than its antithesis, English society) is seen as the actual object of the speaker's examination. The fact that the speaker seems largely oblivious to what he is doing is perhaps the central reason that the nickname "Beppo" becomes an instrument for the pervading irony in the poem rather than merely a term of familiarity. "But why they usher Lent with so much glee in, / Is more than I can tell," the speaker as social critic remarks midway through his preparation for the story, "although I guess / 'Tis as we take a glass with friends at parting, / In the Stage-Coach or Packet, just at starting." The speaker's setting and subject are emphatically particular, but, unknown to him, they become, through irony, general and human.

The speaker assumes the center of attention, which might expectedly be held by the protagonist. Through the first twenty stanzas he digresses, but even the digressions do not form a composite image of a personality or Self, any more than the cosmogony of the protagonist in one of the early Tales becomes a compelling whole. Here, however, failure to organize either the inner or the outer world becomes posi-

tive, the basis for irony. The speaker discusses the differences
between the Catholic Lenten abstention and Protestant indulgence. "A Lent will well nigh starve ye," he remarks, adding the qualification:

> That is to say, if your religion's Roman,
>   And you at Rome would do as Romans do,
> According to the proverb,—although no man,
>   If foreign, is obliged to fast; and you,
> If Protestant, or sickly, or a woman,
>   Would rather dine in sin on a ragout—
> Dine and be d——d! I don't mean to be coarse,
> But that's the penalty, to say no worse.

Emphasizing the particular aspects of such a distinction, he
unwittingly makes us aware of the general, which have been
overlooked, we may infer, by the restrained Protestant society
that experiences neither complete fasting nor full indulgence.
He has unknowingly been "coarse" to this point, in a way
far exceeding his use of the form "d——d" but which a
reader who is either "sickly . . . or a woman" would miss.
In another instance we have the question of the setting of
the poem. The period is first identified as that in which
Venice "was in all her glory" (x), but subsequently it is placed
"some years ago / It may be thirty, forty, more or less" (xxi).
The obvious inconsistency, an aspect of the personality of the
speaker, derives from the poet's method and is not an instance
of his failure. Of sole importance in the setting is Venice itself, the first "Of all the places where the Carnival / Was
most facetious in the days of yore." The speaker's image of it
establishes the atmosphere in which the action of his narrative is to take place. He sees its women resembling "so many
Venuses of Titian's" and in some instances recalling one of
Giorgione's paintings:

> Love in full life and length, not love ideal,
>   No, nor ideal beauty, that fine name,
> But something better still, so very real,
>   That the sweet Model must have been the same;
> A thing that you would purchase, beg, or steal,
>   Wer't not impossible, besides a shame.

The hint concerning the nature of the story he is about to tell, which perhaps he offers unknowingly, is made more specific somewhat later as he traces how "glances beget ogles, ogles sighs, / Sighs wishes, wishes words, and words a letter," leading ultimately to "Vile assignations, and adulterous beds, / Elopements, broken vows, and hearts, and heads." The speaker introduces Desdemona, who significantly was a Venetian, but the emphasis upon Othello's absurdity,

> And to this day from Venice to Verona
>   Such matters may be probably the same,
> Except that since those times was never known a
>   Husband whom mere suspicion could inflame
> To suffocate a wife no more than twenty,
> Because she had a "Cavalier Servente,"

not only reveals quite clearly the kind of story he is going to tell but suggests the way in which he is *not* going to end it.

In the beginning of the narrative itself the speaker's imprecision concerning the setting is extended to the characters. Protesting that he does not know the real name of "A certain lady" about whom he tells, he remarks: "And so we'll call her Laura, if you please, / Because it slips into my verse with ease." It becomes apparent somewhat later that the name of the supposed protagonist, "a merchant trading to Aleppo," has been determined in much the same way. The description of him is merely physical, emphasizing his complexion and thereby anticipating the conclusion of the narrative; but it fully serves its purpose, for in the speaker's story Beppo really does no more than disappear and return. Laura, on the other hand, plays a part that appears to involve choice, so that her moral position must be established: "And she, although her manners showed no rigour, / Was deemed a woman of the strictest principle, / So much as to be thought *almost* invincible" (italics mine). The ironic description of Laura and Beppo's "pathetic" parting ("kneeling on the shore upon her sad knee / He left this Adriatic Ariadne") implicitly recalls the speaker's earlier mention of taking "a glass with friends at parting" and prepares for the bringing together of the two themes of appetite in the next stanza, which is of course reminiscent of that achieved through the ambiguities occurring early in the poem:

> And Laura waited long, and wept a little,
>   And thought of wearing weeds, as well she might;
> She almost lost all appetite for victual,
>   And could not sleep with ease alone at night;
> She deemed the window-frames and shutters brittle
>   Against a daring housebreaker or sprite,
> And so she thought it prudent to connect her
> With a vice-husband, *chiefly* to *protect her.*

The apparent but incredible naïveté of the speaker fully emerges in the ironically protracted description of the Count's social qualities, which concludes: "In short, he was a perfect Cavaliero, / And to his very valet seemed a hero."

In describing the ideal Cavalier Servente, the speaker, as we might expect, assumes a supposedly English viewpoint, showing appropriate moral restraint, vastly simplifying what he discusses ("within the Alps, to every woman," though sinful, "'Tis, I may say, permitted to have *two* men"), and concluding with the fear that the institution might be exported: "But Heaven preserve Old England from such courses! / Or what becomes of damage and divorces?" The transition from the discussion of the Cavalier Servente to that of the beauty of Italy is not so abrupt as might first appear, for the theme of both is the certainty of Nature's fulfillment in Italy as opposed, by constant implication and occasional assertion, to the situation in England. In his catalogue of the glories of Italy, the speaker in several stanzas reaches Italian women: "I like the women too (forgive my folly!)" He has come full cycle from his digression upon the women of Venice. Now, after a brief summing up of his praise of Italy, he makes explicit what has therein been ironically implied as the object of his concern:

> "England! with all thy faults I love thee still,"
>   I said at Calais, and have not forgot it;
> I like to speak and lucubrate my fill;
>   I like the government (but that is not it);
> I like the freedom of the press and quill;
>   I like the Habeas Corpus (when we've got it);
> I like a Parliamentary debate,
> Particularly when 'tis not too late.
>
> I like the taxes, when they're not too many;
>   I like a seacoal fire, when not too dear;
> I like a beef-steak, too, as well as any;
>   Have no objection to a pot of beer;
> I like the weather,—when it is not rainy,
>   That is, I like two months of every year.
> And so God save the Regent, Church, and King!
> Which means that I like all and every thing.

Now ready to resume his narrative, the speaker apologizes for digression ("a sin, that by degrees / Becomes exceeding tedious to my mind, / And, therefore, may the reader too displease") and immediately thereafter digresses once more: upon the appearance of Laura, the meaning of the phrase "mixed company," the nature of the *grand monde* in England, the possible Divinity of Fortune, and finally the crowd at the Ridotto (to which Laura and her Count go for an evening during the Carnival). Gradually, with all the discussion of style and fashion, Laura herself has come to the center of the attention of the speaker and his audience; about her the ensuing action in the tale, what little there is, shall revolve. This involves the interest shown her by the mysterious Turk, whose identity is unknown to Laura though at least suspected by the audience. At this point, which is presumably the climax of the action in the simple narrative, the speaker turns away from his story and lectures upon the Turks' treatment of their wives (which, though the speaker seems to be unaware of the fact, is strikingly unlike Beppo's use of Laura), English "Blues," and contemporary writers. In the remainder of his story the narrator reveals the same artlessness that has been his throughout. After recounting Beppo's revelation of his identity, for example, he digresses momentarily upon the difference between Turkish and European coffee.

The tale of Beppo's own adventure becomes a travesty of others of its kind, those of Lara and Mazeppa as well as that of the Ancient Mariner:

> He was cast away
> About where Troy stood once, and nothing stands;
>   Became a slave *of course,* and for his pay
> Had bread and bastinadoes, till some bands
>   Of pirates landing in a neighboring bay,
> He joined the rogues and prospered, and became
> A renegado of indifferent fame
>
> (italics mine)

Growing rich and nostalgic, Beppo decided that, despite risks, he would return home. After he had succeeded, he drew conclusions, which the speaker now reports: "*He* said that

Providence protected him— / For my part, I say nothing— lest we clash / In our opinions." Beppo "landed to reclaim" what was no longer as she had been to him, "His wife," and what had never been lost, either theologically or legally, his "religion, house, and Christian name." Paradoxically, then, "His wife received, the Patriarch re-baptised him." The speaker closes with a sketch of Beppo's later years, remarking with no apparent self-consciousness that he himself does not believe half of the stories told by Beppo and concluding with a comment upon his own chief fault: "here [at the end of a page] the story ends: / 'Tis to be wished it had been sooner done, / But stories somehow lengthen when begun."

ii

The suggestion that *Don Juan* is constructed largely upon the use of dramatic irony, which the poet began to use early in his career and developed more or less consistently thereafter, runs counter to the dominant tendency in Byron criticism.[3] Many of those who have written about the poem have regarded nearly all utterances in the first person as primarily, and often exclusively, Byron's own. Such a viewpoint arises from excessive literalness in particular instances and from a basic failure to understand the structure of the poem; on occasion it has led critics toward the quest for such values as "sincerity" and perhaps even "consistency."

In most instances the speaker refers to situations or events which Byron actually experienced or observed, and it is perfectly reasonable in a study of the whole being of the poem to point to these and in fact to explore all possibilities of autobiographical reference; this approach is obviously necessary if we are to appreciate the poem as Byron's contemporaries did. But in various cases we know that the speaker cannot have been Byron in his own person. An obvious example

is found in that section of the first canto (ccix-ccxi) in which
the speaker reports that for a favorable review of the poem
he has "bribed my grandmother's review—the British"; William Roberts, editor of *The British Review,* confusing the
poet and a persona, emphatically denied that he had received
a bribe.[4] Roberts is not to be condemned, however, for he
was simply one of the first (and he certainly had a more compelling reason than most) who failed to comprehend the
structure of *Don Juan.* To insist in all instances upon the
autobiographical aspect of the speaker's utterance leads along
some false paths; to insist in any instance upon an exclusively
autobiographical approach to the poem deprives us of the
opportunity to understand what is happening at that point
and throughout the poem as a whole. Lady Pinchbeck, to
use an easy example, may be cast in the image of Lady Mel-
bourne or Lady Blessington,[5] but she is also a significantly
ironic figure, a fact that has hardly been recognized.

Some may seek a basis for the assurance of unity in the
poem by looking at the tale itself rather than by making extensive biographical correlation. Set amid digression, the narrative in *Don Juan* reminds us, for rather different reasons,
of Dr. Johnson's remark about Richardson's novels: "Why,
sir, if you were to read Richardson for the story, your impa-
tience would be so much fretted that you would hang your-
self." Unlike *Pamela* and *Clarissa,* Byron's poem cannot of
course be read for its moral. We approach the hero, seeking
that force whose dominance will give unity to the work. What
we find is totally ironic. Taken from a tradition of strong
heroes, he, like the Anglicized form that is pointedly given
his name, is sufficiently altered to be merely a mockery of the
prototype. From the speaker's original announcement, "I
want a hero," and his decision to take a traditional hero because the present age offers neither heroes nor heroism, it is
ironically apparent that this protagonist is especially unhe-

roic. Like Beppo and unlike the many possible French heroes whose names are recited early in the first canto (ii-iii), Don Juan is ostensibly chosen for one reason, the potential for rhyme which his name offers. The identity of Juan is insubstantial and he himself is essentially passive, the victim or instrument of persons and situations in all that he encounters. In *Don Juan* the poet created an ironic image of the protagonist in his own poems of the Early and Middle Phases,[6] indeed the "Donny Johnny" to whom Byron in his letters occasionally referred.

What then is left? Only the seeming myriad of speakers in the poem. For long sections, occurring more frequently as the poem progresses, the narrative and its protagonist are unceremoniously abandoned. One after another, in sequence or in conflict, the various speakers emerge. Some readers have complained that the principal fault of *Don Juan* is its lack of consistency. This is, instead, its dominant virtue in terms of what it is supposed to do and what it does. At one moment the speaker emerging is naïve, prudish, perhaps stupid; he may be prudent to the point of absurdity, sometimes concerned with exasperating details, elsewhere frightened at the implications of what he recounts. At other times, however, the speaker is worldly, indiscreet, perhaps cynical. Frequently the form assumed by the speaker represents the antithesis of the nature of the action that he recounts (in moments of intensified sexuality he displays extraordinary prudishness), and on other occasions, as in his preparations to describe battle in the eighth canto, he himself imposes the mood upon the narrative. At the moment of tension a speaker interrupts and comments most inappropriately: during the scene in Donna Julia's bedroom, the shipwreck, the touching moments of Juan and Haidée. Tension is relieved. We seek no surprises; nor do we seek answers. What was serious now appears ludicrous. On occasion two speakers may be juxtaposed:

in the third canto one makes an emphatic attack upon Wordsworth (xcviii-c), only to be followed several stanzas later (civ-cvi) by another emerging rather unobtrusively who utters what must clearly be taken as an imitation or a parody of Wordsworth: "My altars are the mountains and the ocean, / Earth, air, stars,—all that springs from the great Whole, / Who hath produced, and will receive the soul." The use of various speakers, ironic and among each other inconsistent, to comment upon the method and structure of the poem is perhaps too abundant and in many instances too obvious to require illustration.

In their dramatic function, in *how* they say rather than in *what* they say, the speakers in *Don Juan* achieve the irony that dominates the poem, thereby intensifying what is revealed in its panoramic view: the imperfection in Man's powers, the acute limitations upon what he can achieve for himself, and in fact the impossibility of his achieving an integrated and continuous view of the Self and therefore of the world upon which that Self must impose meaning. *Don Juan* should be regarded as a vast literary joke (some have called it a farce), which is humorous in its means but, beneath the clownish leer, serious in its implications. It is not satire, for it ultimately offers, in its description of the absurdities of the real, no suggestion of the ideal. Its irony is terminal rather than instrumental; this is achieved and sustained principally through a complex of individual monologues, in which the speakers, often unaware of the full situational context for their speeches, frequently reveal to us far more than they intend.

Notes to Chapter One

[1] "Lord Byron," *The Compete Works of William Hazlitt*, ed. P. P. Howe (21 vols.; London, 1932), XI, 74.

[2] One of the more recent instances is that of Mr. Paul West, who opens his book, *Byron and the Spoiler's Art* (New York, 1960, p. 11), with the assertion, "The pageant of the bleeding heart has run dry"; but regarding Byron as essentially a cathartic poet, West necessarily derives opinions of the poems from biographical judgments, concluding that *Don Juan* is the most successful poem Byron wrote because it is the most complete expression of the urge toward "elimination."

[3] In his edition, *The Works of Lord Byron: Poetry* (7 vols.; London, 1898-1904), Ernest Hartley Coleridge erred on occasion in this direction. Commenting upon Byron's use of one of Lucifer's speeches in *Cain*, Coleridge remarked, "The *spirit* of error, not the Manichaean heresy, should have proceeded out of his lips" (V, 254).

[4] "Byron," *A History of Western Philosophy* (New York, 1945), pp. 746-52.

[5] "Byron," *On Poetry and Poets* (New York, 1937, 1957). This essay has been reprinted perhaps most accessibly in *English Romantic Poets: Modern Essays in Criticism*, ed. M. H. Abrams (New York, 1960), pp. 196-209.

[6] Byron to Robert Charles Dallas, January 21, 1808 (*The Works of Lord Byron: Letters and Journals*, ed. Rowland E. Prothero [6 vols.; London, 1898-1901], I, 173).

[7] His position is that which Morse Peckham ("Toward a Theory of Romanticism," *PMLA*, LXVI [1951], 5-23) finds characteristic of *negative romanticism*, defined as "the expression of the attitudes, the feelings, and the ideas of a man who has left static mechanism but has not yet arrived at a reintegration of his thought and art in terms of dynamic organicism." Static mechanism obviously demands an absolute view of the universe; dynamic organicism, in that it accepts (in fact, presupposes) growth and change, is a form of what we might call relativism.

[8] See Ernest J. Lovell, Jr., *Byron: The Record of a Quest* (Austin, 1949)—a book to which obviously I am in many ways indebted for suggestions relating to the problems discussed here.

[9] For the most comprehensive discussion of this matter, see Ernest J. Lovell, Jr., "Irony and Image in Byron's *Don Juan*," *The Major English Romantic Poets: A Symposium in Reappraisal*, ed. Clarence D. Thorpe, Carlos Baker, Bennett Weaver (Carbondale, Ill., 1957), pp. 129-48; reprinted, *English Romantic Poets*, ed. Abrams, pp. 228-46.

[10] *The Classical Tradition in Poetry* (New York, 1957), p. 51.

[11] *The Well-Wrought Urn: Studies in the Structure of Poetry* (New York, 1947), p. 208.

[12] For an assertion of an extreme position regarding the necessary distinction between the personality and the artist, see Charles DuBos, *Byron et le Besoin de la Fatalité*, trans. Ethel Colburn Mayne (London, 1932), pp. 159-60, 161.

179

¹³ This is the first volume of *Byron's Don Juan: A Variorum Edition*, ed. Truman Guy Steffan and Willis W. Pratt (4 vols.; Austin, 1957).

¹⁴ One of the clearest discussions of the problem, to which I am obviously indebted though with which I disagree in many particulars, is Robert Penn Warren's Introduction to his edition of Coleridge's *The Rime of the Ancient Mariner* (New York, 1946).

¹⁵ A chronological list of Byron's major poems follows:

Title	Written	Printed or Published
[Early poems]	1802 ff.	
Fugitive Pieces		1806
Poems on Various Occasions		1807
Hours of Idleness		1807
Poems Original and Translated		1808
English Bards and Scotch Reviewers	1808	1809
Childe Harold's Pilgrimage, I and *II*	1809-10	1812
Hints from Horace	1811	1811 (proofs) 1831
The Curse of Minerva	1811	1812 (private) 1815
The Waltz	1812	1813
The Giaour: A Fragment of a Turkish Tale	1813	1813
The Corsair: A Tale	1813	1814
Ode to Napoleon Buonaparte	1814	1816
Lara: A Tale	1814	1814
Hebrew Melodies	1814-15	1815
The Siege of Corinth; Parisina	1815	1816 (1 volume)
Childe Harold's Pilgrimage, III	1816	1816
The Prisoner of Chillon	1816	1816
Manfred: A Dramatic Poem	1816	1817
The Lament of Tasso	1817	1817
Childe Harold's Pilgrimage, IV	1817	1818
Beppo	1817	1818
Mazeppa	1818	1819
Don Juan, I and *II*	1818-19	1819
The Morgante Maggiore of Pulci	1819-20	1823
Don Juan, III-V	1819-20	1821
The Prophecy of Dante; Marino Faliero, Doge of Venice: An Historical Tragedy	1819, 1820	1821 (1 volume
Sardanapalus: A Tragedy; The Two Foscari: An Historical Tragedy; Cain: A Mystery	1821	1821 (1 volume)
The Vision of Judgment	1821	1822
The Blues: A Literary Eclogue	1821	1823
Heaven and Earth: A Mystery	1821	1823
Werner; or, The Inheritance: A Tragedy	1821-22	1822
The Deformed Transformed: A Drama	1822	1824
Don Juan, VI-VIII	1822	1823
Don Juan, IX-XI	1822	1823

The Age of Bronze; or, Carmen Seculare	1822-23	1823
et Annus Haud Mirabilis		
Don Juan, XII-XIV	1822-23	1823
The Island; or, Christian and His Comrades	1823	1823
Don Juan, XV-XVI	1823	1824
Don Juan, XVII (i-xiv)	1823	1903

[16] Brooks, p. 213.

[17] *The Prisoner of Chillon* and *Mazeppa* have been traditionally regarded merely as Tales. Ernest Bernbaum (*Guide through the Romantic Movement* [New York, 1949], p. 200) pointed out that the first of these is a dramatic monologue, but then continued with the traditional interpretation of the poem: "he [Byron] illustrated the sufferings which those have endured who tried to liberate mankind from oppression.

[18] See William H. Marshall, "The Accretive Structure of Byron's 'The Giaour,'" *Modern Language Notes*, LXXVI (1961), 502-9.

[19] William J. Calvert (*Byron, The Romantic Paradox* [Chapel Hill, 1935]) assumes the position that Byron's work deteriorated to the level of the romances of 1813 and 1814 but rose again after the crisis of 1816 had forced Byron from the artificial world in which he had been living and his grief renewed in him sincerity and self-knowledge.

[20] After much deliberation I have omitted consideration of *The Vision of Judgment*, which falls outside the main course of Byron's development and, despite its obvious effectiveness, owes but little to the techniques which he employed, with generally increasing success, in his major poetry.

Notes to Chapter Two

[1] Less familiar to literary students than other objects of the speaker's scorn, James Grahame (1765-1811) was a lawyer who was later ordained. In his note Byron described him as one who "has poured forth two volumes of Cant, under the name of *Sabbath Walks* and *Biblical Pictures*" (*Poetry*, I, 323).

[2] Byron's impression of the affair is given in his note: "In 1806, Messrs. Jeffrey and Moore met at Chalk Farm. The duel was prevented by the interference of the Magistracy; and on examination, the balls of the pistols were found to have evaporated. This incident gave occasion to much waggery in the daily prints" (*Poetry*, I, 333).

Notes to Chapter Three

[1] See *Poetry*, III, 443-44, 499-500.

[2] Except for one instance (*Letters and Journals*, VI, 81), Byron's published remarks about *Lara* concern matters of publication and of public reaction.

[3] George Agar Ellis ("Lord Byron's *Corsair* and *Lara*," *The Quarterly Review*, XI [1814], 453) easily concluded that in *Lara* "the high-minded and generous Conrad, who had preferred death and torture to life and liberty, if purchased by a nightly liberty, is degraded into a vile and cowardly assassin." An American critic ("Lara, A Tale," *The Port-Folio*, Series 3, VI

[1815], 49) tended less toward explicit accusation, merely paraphrasing the account in the poem of the prevailing attitude toward Lara: "Suspicion has grown almost into belief, that he was the cause of this Ezzelin's sudden disappearance: for who but Lara could have reason to fear his presence? who made him disappear, if not the man on whom his threatened charge would otherwise have rested too deeply?" Recently Robert Escarpit (*Lord Byron: Un Tempérament Littéraire* [2 vols.; Paris, 1957], II, 206-7) has remarked: "On ne saura plus jamais rien de la disparition d'Ezzelin, sauf ce qu'a vu un serf attardé une nuit près de la riv[i]ère qui sépare le domaine de Lara de celui d'Othon: un cavalier masqué jetant dans l'eau le cadavre d'un chevalier. Ce n'est qu'ainsi qu'on pourra soupçonner le crime de Lara." Whether Escarpit means to cast doubt upon Lara's guilt or to insist upon the reality of "le crime de Lara" despite limited reason for suspicion is not clear. If the former is the case, he has not pursued the suggestion and has failed to show that to do so would be to establish a possible basis for relation of the two elements that are most important in the story, the matter of Kaled's sex and the murder of Ezzelin. Instead, proposing that the narrative structure of *The Corsair* reveals a weakening from that of *The Giaour* and *The Bride of Abydos*, Escarpit concludes: "Le décor vaguement lunaire de *Lara* ne fait que favoriser cette tendance. Il n'y a en fait presque plus rien de narratif dans cette suite insatisfaisante du *Corsair*."

⁴ *The Oxford Companion to English Literature*, ed. Sir Paul Harvey (Oxford, 1940), p. 444.

⁵ An example is the suggestion that Kaled's disguise as a page is derived in large measure from Lady Caroline Lamb's use of that in 1812 as a means of gaining admittance to Byron's chambers.

⁶ This fact was emphasized by E. H. Coleridge in his introduction to *Lara* (*Poetry*, III, 320), but he did not develop the implications of the equation of characters.

⁷ One example is the passage describing Lara's actions while he is alone in the hall (I, 181-200), matters which the speaker could not really know. It may reveal something of Byron's growing conception of the structure of *Lara* and of his general awareness of this fault in the poem that one of the additions made after the completion of the poem was the passage (II, 1099-1134) in which the speaker is partly identified (see *Poetry*, III, 364 n).

⁸ For an excellent discussion of the relations of Lara and other Byronic heroes to their class, one to which I am indebted but with which obviously I do not entirely agree, see Carl Lefevre, "Lord Byron's Fiery Convert of Revenge," *Studies in Philology*, XLIX (1952), 468-87.

⁹ *Poetry*, III, 500.

¹⁰ Otto Rank (*Das Inzest-Motiv in Dichtung und Sage* [Leipzig und Wien, 1926], pp. 138-43) discussed some of these, but he was concerned with them primarily as symptoms of Byron's own emotional situation at the time that he wrote the poem. Psychographic criticism of literature derives from the thesis of Freud (*Introductory Lectures on Psycho-Analysis* [London, 1922], pp. 314-15) that art is essentially an elaboration of the daydream, a projection of impulses buried deep within the artist. This concept reduces art to the status of clinical evidence, however, and criticism to an analysis of the artist through his work. It contains the denial of biographical criticism, that is, that

we study the life of an artist so that we might better understand his work, for this approach moves in the opposite direction for ultimately diagnostic purposes: it essentially reveals nothing about the work itself. There is, however, a clear place for psychoanalytic criticism, which fits within many of the accepted systems for the historical and critical study of literature and, in fact, rests upon one of the most traditional of assumptions, that one form of literary art is a direct imitation of life. Those writers working with this form successfully in the past have been familiar, in part unconsciously so, with human motives and actions, now explained and in some sense defined by the psychologist, and have brought this familiarity to their work. To use psychoanalytic methods to examine the character motivations and consequently the structure of a given piece of literature is not to imply that the author was in any anachronistic way "psychoanalytic." It is merely to employ an instrument at hand for useful purposes.

¹¹ E. H. Coleridge (*Poetry*, III, 516) complained that in lines 234-40, though the meaning is clear, "the construction is involved." He regarded it merely as "one of Byron's curious infelicities," but such, I think, is not the case.

¹² That Byron was aware of the essential structural substitution of the personality of Parisina for the image of Bianca is at least suggested by his comparison of the scream to "a mother's o'er her child, / Done to death by sudden blow" (490-91). Earlier in the poem he has described Parisina as "The living cause of Hugo's ill" (327), compared by implication with Bianca, the *dead* cause.

Notes to Chapter Four

¹ Fifty-five Spenserian stanzas precede the four ten-line stanzas of "The castled Crag of Drachenfels," totaling fifty-nine stanzas in the first part of the poem, in which Harold is a reality; sixty-three Spenserian stanzas follow. Approximate mechanical balance appears in this manner to give support to the organic regularity of the poem.

² An analysis of the mechanical structure of *The Prisoner of Chillon* reveals very little. The seventh, eighth, tenth, twelfth, and thirteenth stanzas are principally narrative, and the others are primarily descriptive. With the exception of the twelfth stanza, those which are narrative are generally longer than the others: i (26 lines), ii (21), iii (21), iv (23), v (15), vi (19), vii (38), viii (67), ix (20), x (49), xi (18), xii (14), xiii (35), xiv (27).

³ E. H. Coleridge's note (*Poetry*, IV, 19) on the lines following offers an irresistible example of the unfortunate results of a reading of this poem which, taking Byron literally in his Preface and the "Sonnet," identifies the speaker and Bonnivard: "The 'real Bonivard' might have indulged in and, perhaps, prided himself on this feeble and irritating *paranomasy;* but nothing can be less in keeping with the bearing and behaviour of the tragic and sententious Bonivard of the legend.

⁴ On two occasions (lines 228, 351-52) E. H. Coleridge (IV, 22, 27) notes parallels between *The Prisoner of Chillon* and *The Ancient Mariner*. In themselves these should not appear surprising if the point is made that from the aspect of the structure of the poems and the psychological situation and philosophic problem of the speakers, *The Ancient Mariner* and *The Prisoner*

of Chillon are impressively similar. See Lionel Stevenson, " 'The Ancient Mariner' as a Dramatic Monologue," *The Personalist*, XXX (1949), 34-44; William H. Marshall, "Coleridge, the Mariner, and Dramatic Irony," *Ibid.*, XLII (1961), 524-32.

Notes to Chapter Five

[1] Samuel C. Chew (*The Dramas of Lord Byron: A Critical Study* [Baltimore, 1915], p. 52) regarded the play as the dramatization of spiritual triumph rather than of psychological adjustment to emotional failure: "*Manfred* is, from one point of view, a continued growth of power over the spiritual world; defiance, first of the spirits of the earth, then of the evil principle itself, then of death.

[2] Chew, p. 52.

Notes to Chapter Six

[1] Byron made no comment on the question of the justice of Tasso's confinement. In the "Advertisement" to the poem he remarked, somewhat enigmatically, that at the hospital of St. Anna, where Tasso had been confined, "there are two inscriptions, one on the outer gate, the second over the cell itself, inviting, unnecessarily, the wonder and the indignation of the spectator" (*Poetry*, IV, 139).

[2] The last line recalls one in the third stanza (65), in which Tasso made the contrast between the "maniac cry" and his own reasoned utterance at the time that both the maniac and he were beset by their tyrants. Perhaps we can extend this comparison between the third and seventh stanzas somewhat, particularly since the fifth stanza, in which Tasso describes his love for Leonora, is, from the conscious viewpoint of the speaker, of central significance. The opening and closing stanzas reveal several obvious parallels, as do the second and eighth in their concern for "decay," and the fourth and sixth as primary expressions of the messianic impulse.

[3] For a discussion of the early criticism of *Mazeppa*, see E. Kölbing's review "D. Englaender, Lord Byron's Mazeppa," *Englische Studien*, XXIV (1898), 448-5

[4] That Charles does not regard Mazeppa with full seriousness is at least suggested by his presumably ironic remark, "So fit a pair had never birth, / Since Alexander's day till now, / As thy Bucephalus and thou" (102-4). According to the *O. E. D.*, the term "Bucephalus" was at this time applied "humorously as a name for any riding horse."

[5] Here, as in the case of *The Prisoner of Chillon*, the analogy between the state of the protagonist and that of the Ancient Mariner, which E. H. Coleridge has indicated (IV, 225), is very much to the point.

[6] In his "Preface" to the poem Byron wrote: "The reader is requested to suppose that Dante addresses him in the interval between the conclusion of the *Divina Commedia* and his death, and shortly before the latter event, foretelling the fortunes of Italy in general in the ensuing centuries" (*Poetry*, IV, 243).

[7] E. H. Coleridge (IV, 256) points to the similarity between this apostrophe to Italy and the *Purgatorio* (vi, 76-127).

[8] Dante is here speaking within character and should not be identified with Byron, as E. H. Coleridge proposed (IV, 265): "If Byron had lived half a century later, he might have placed Ariosto and Tasso after and not before Petrarch."

Notes to Chapter Seven

[1] This adaptation of the Manichaean thesis explains parts of the play which otherwise prove difficult or impossible. The theme itself is the principal means by which *Cain* achieves structural unity. Edward E. Bostetter, in a recent consideration of the play, "Byron and the Politics of Paradise," *PMLA*, LXXV (1960), 571-76, found structural problems which recognition of the theme would presumably solve. For this reason *Cain* appears to be far more heretical than perhaps its most violent critics in Byron's day suspected.

[2] Byron wrote only Part I, which was published in *The Liberal*, I (1822-23), 165-206. He was reported by Thomas Medwin (*Journal of the Conversations of Lord Byron* [London, 1824], pp. 155-57) to have outlined his intentions regarding Part II.

[3] Each was subtitled "A Mystery," both were written in 1821, and John Murray's unwillingness to publish *Heaven and Earth* arose from the difficulties he encountered as the publisher of *Cain*.

[4] Stopford Brooke ("Byron's *Cain*," *The Hibbert Journal*, XVIII [1919], 74) pointed rather emphatically to the supposed anti-Calvinism in *Cain*, but he made no reference to *Heaven and Earth*.

[5] E. H. Coleridge (*Poetry*, V, 309)

Notes to Chapter Eight

[1] See E. H. Coleridge's introduction to *Beppo* (*Poetry*, IV, 155-58) and Steffan, *The Making of a Masterpiece*.

[2] E.g., "fiddling" (I, 7), "gallants" (II, 6), "strumming" (II, 8), "gymnastical" (III, 3), "flesh" (VI, 2), "fish both salt and fresh" (VI, 4), "carnal dishes" (VII, 1), "meats" (VII, 2), "sauces" (VII, 4), "stews" (VII, 4), and numerous others, which are considered in *Slang and Its Analogues Past and Present*, ed. John S. Farmer and W. E. Henley (7 vols.; London, 1890-1904). Perhaps in time a thorough study will be made of Byron's use of slang and its analogues, particularly in *Beppo* and *Don Juan*. The problems involving semantic change would be numerous, and the value of an extensive investigation, except to intensify critical awareness of one aspect of Byron's ironic techniques in these later poems, remains somewhat doubtful.

[3] The principal exception, already mentioned, is Lovell's "Irony and Image in Byron's *Don Juan*," an essay which is indispensable to any critical consideration of the poem and to which in the present remarks I am obviously indebted.

[4] For a discussion of the Roberts affair, see William H. Marshall, *Byron, Shelley, Hunt, and The Liberal* (Philadelphia, 1960).

⁸ See *Byron's Don Juan: A Variorum Edition,* IV, 240.

⁹ The reason for which Don Juan is chosen as protagonist may recall the incidental purpose for which, according to the Preface to the first two cantos of *Childe Harold's Pilgrimage,* Byron gave the name "Childe" to his hero. In the earlier instance the admission of the poet suggested weakness in the poem; in the later, however, the speaker's indication of what he has done simply intensifies the ironic quality of the poem. As others have pointed out, Juan is merely Harold seen in an entirely different light.

Bibliography

In this list, which is composed principally of works mentioned in the footnotes, I have not included many of the books and articles with which a Byron scholar may be assumed to be familiar and which necessarily constitute the background for any study of Byron's poetry. Only the titles of biographical studies which have made a direct contribution, therefore, appear here.

Abrams, M. H. (ed.). *English Romantic Poets: Modern Essays in Criticism.* New York: Oxford University Press, 1960.

Bernbaum, Ernest. *Guide through the Romantic Movement.* New York: The Ronald Press, 1949.

Bostetter, Edward E. "Byron and the Politics of Paradise," *PMLA,* LXXV (1960), 571-7

Boyd, Elizabeth French. *Byron's Don Juan. A Critical Study.* New Brunswick, New Jersey: Rutgers University Press, 1945.

Brooke, Stopford. "Byron's Cain," *The Hibbert Journal,* XVIII (1919), 74-94.

Brooks, Cleanth. *The Well-Wrought Urn: Studies in the Structure of Poetry.* New York: Harcourt, Brace and Company, 1947.

Byron, Lord. *Works: Poetry,* ed. E. H. Coleridge. 7 vols.; *Letters and Journals,* ed. R. E. Prothero. 6 vols. London: John Murray, 1898-1903.

Calvert, William J. *Byron, The Romantic Paradox.* Chapel Hill: University of North Carolina Press, 1935.

Chew, Samuel C. *The Dramas of Lord Byron.* Baltimore: Johns Hopkins University Press, 1915.

DuBos, Charles. *Byron et le Besoin de la Fatalité.* Translated by Ethel Colburn Mayne. London: Putnam, 1932.

Eliot, T. S. *On Poetry and Poets.* New York: Farrar, Straus and Cudahy, 1937, 1957.

Escarpit, Robert. *Lord Byron. Un Tempérament Littéraire.* 2 vols. Paris: Le Cercle du Livre, 1957.

Fuess, Claude M. *Lord Byron as a Satirist in Verse.* New York: Columbia University Press, 1912.

Harvey, Sir Paul. *The Oxford Companion to English Literature.* Oxford: The Clarendon Press, 1940.

Hazlitt, William. *The Complete Works,* ed. P. P. Howe. 21 vols. London and Toronto: J. M. Dent & Sons, 1930-34.

Kölbing, E. "D. Englaender, Lord Byron's Mazeppa," *Englische Studien,* XXIV (1898), 448-58.

Lefevre, Carl. "Lord Byron's Fiery Convert of Revenge," *Studies in Philology,* XLIX (1952), 468-87.

Lovell, Ernest J., Jr. *Byron: The Record of a Quest.* Austin: University of Texas Press, 1949.

———. "Irony and Image in Byron's *Don Juan,*" *The Major English Roman-*

tic Poets: A Symposium in Reappraisal, ed. Clarence D. Thorpe, Carlos Baker, Bennett Weaver. Carbondale, Ill.: Southern Illinois University Press, 1957.

Marshall, William H. "The Accretive Structure of Byron's 'The Giaour,'" *Modern Language Notes*, LXXVI (1961), 502-9.

————. *Byron, Shelley, Hunt, and The Liberal*. Philadelphia: University of Pennsylvania Press, 1960

————. "Byron's *Parisina* and the Function of Psychoanalytic Criticism," *The Personalist*, XLII (1961), 213-23.

————. "Coleridge, The Mariner, and Dramatic Irony," *The Personalist*, XLII (1961), 524-32.

————. "A Reading of Byron's *Mazeppa*," *Modern Language Notes*, LXXVI (1961), 120-24.

Medwin, Thomas. *Journal of the Conversations of Lord Byron: Noted during a Residence with His Lordship at Pisa, in the Years 1821 and 1822*. London: Henry Colburn, 1824.

Murray, Gilbert. *The Classical Tradition in Poetry*. New York: Vintage Press, 1957.

Peckham, Morse. "Toward a Theory of Romanticism," *PMLA*, LXVI (1951), 5-23.

Pratt, Willis W., and Steffan, Truman Guy (eds.). *Byron's Don Juan: A Variorum Edition*. 4 vols. Austin: University of Texas Press, 1957.

Rank, Otto. *Das Inzest-Motiv in Dichtung und Sage*. Leipzig und Wien: F. Deuticke, 1926.

Robson, W. W. *Byron as Poet*. London: Oxford University Press, 1958.

Russell, Bertrand. *A History of Western Philosophy*. New York: Simon and Schuster, 1945.

Stevenson, Lionel. "'The Ancient Mariner' as a Dramatic Monologue," *The Personalist*, XXX (1949), 34-44.

Trueblood, Paul G. *The Flowering of Byron's Genius: Studies in Byron's Don Juan*. Stanford: Stanford University Press, 1945.

Warren, Robert Penn (ed.). *The Rime of the Ancient Mariner by Samuel Taylor Coleridge*. New York: Reynal & Hitchcock, 1946.

West, Paul. *Byron and the Spoiler's Art*. New York: St. Martin's Press, 1960.

Index

Unless otherwise indicated, all poems indexed are Byron's.